OUR FATHER WHICH ART IN HEAVEN,
HALLOWED BE THY NAME.
THY KINGDOM COME.
THY WILL BE DONE IN EARTH, AS IT IS IN HEAVEN.
GIVE US THIS DAY OUR DAILY BREAD.
AND FORGIVE US OUR DEBTS,
AS WE FORGIVE OUR DEBTORS.
AND LEAD US NOT INTO TEMPTATION,
BUT DELIVER US FROM EVIL:
FOR THINE IS THE KINGDOM,
AND THE POWER, AND THE GLORY,
FOR EVER. AMEN

Overcoming Your Inner Barriers
to Intimacy with God

SOMETIMES IT'S HARD TO LOVE GOD.

Dennis Guernsey

InterVarsity Press is the book-publishing division of Inter-Varsity Christian Fellowship, a student movement active on campus at hundreds of universities, colleges and schools of nursing. For information about local and regional activities, write Public Relations Dept., InterVarsity Christian Fellowship, 6400 Schroeder Rd., P.O. Box 7895, Madison, WI 53707-7895.

Distributed in Canada through InterVarsity Press, 860 Denison St., Unit 3, Markham, Ontario L3R 4H1, Canada.

All Scripture quotations, unless otherwise indicated, are from the Holy Bible, New International Version. Copyright © 1973, 1978, International Bible Society. Used by permission of Zondervan Bible Publishers.

Quotations from the Lord's Prayer are from the King James (Authorized) Version.

"The Death of the Hired Man," by Robert Frost. Copyright 1930 by Holt, Rinehart and Winston and renewed 1958 by Robert Frost. Reprinted from The Poetry of Robert Frost, edited by Edward Connery Lathem by permission of Henry Holt and Company, Inc.

ISBN 0-8308-1257-1

Printed in the United States of America.

Library of Congress Cataloging-in-Publication Data

Guernsey, Dennis B.
    Sometimes it's hard to love God: overcoming your inner barriers
    to intimacy with God/Dennis Guernsey.
        p.   cm.
    ISBN 0-8308-1257-1
    1. God—Worship and love. 2. Lord's prayer. I. Title.
    BV4817.G813   1989
    242'.722—dc20   89-15306
                                                      CIP

16	15	14	13	12	11	10	9	8	7	6	5	4	3	2	1
99	98	97	96	95	94	93	92	91	90	89					

1/ **W**HEN WE FEEL LIKE SPIRITUAL FAILURES ———————— 7

2/ **W**HEN WE'RE NOT WHAT WE PRETEND TO BE ———————— *15*

3/ **W**HEN OUR UNDERSTANDING OF GOD IS STILL THAT OF A CHILD — *29*
   "Our Father . . ."

4/ **W**HEN OUR EARTHLY EXPERIENCES ARE TOO PAINFUL ———— *37*
   "Which art in heaven . . ."

5/ **W**HEN WE HAVE TROUBLE WITH AUTHORITY ———————— *51*
   "Hallowed be thy name."

6/ **W**HEN OUR MINDS ARE CONFUSED ———————————— *65*
   "Thy kingdom come."

7/ **W**HEN OUR LIVES ARE DIRECTIONLESS ———————————— *79*
   "Thy will be done in earth, as it is in heaven."

8/ **W**HEN WE DON'T KNOW HOW TO ASK ———————————— *89*
   "Give . . . this day . . ."

9/ **W**HEN WE FEEL LONELY ———————————————— *105*
   "Us . . . our . . ."

10/ **W**HEN OUR WORLD IS CONFUSING _____ *117*
  "Daily bread."

11/ **W**HEN WE LIVE WITH UNFORGIVENESS _____ *129*
  "And forgive us our debts, as we forgive our debtors."

12/ **W**HEN WE STRUGGLE WITH SIN _____ *149*
  "And lead us not into temptation, but deliver us from evil . . ."

13/ **A** CLOSING HYMN _____ *165*
  *"For thine is the kingdom, and the power, and the glory,
  for ever. Amen."*

CHAPTER ONE

WHEN
WE FEEL
LIKE SPIRITUAL
FAILURES

*F*requent flyers like me can have interesting experiences on their travels. One time a young mother and her two very young children were flying on the same plane as I was. When it came time to board, the airline personnel announced their usual invitation for those needing assistance to come to the gate for pre-boarding. The young mother didn't hear the announcement, probably due to her naiveté about airports and airplanes. So, rather than board ahead of time, she was in line with the rest of us, trying to herd her two active children and carry her excess baggage. She was having a hard time managing their excitement and her anxiety.

Another business traveler and I observed her situation and offered to help. I ended up with a two-year-old boy holding on to my one hand, with my own briefcase, a garment bag and a bag filled with toys for the trip draped around the other. My fellow Good Samaritan ended up with two extra diaper bags. The mother went on ahead with the other child in her arms plus two additional pieces of miscellaneous paraphernalia. We must have created quite a sight because the line parted as we moved down the ramp to the plane.

It turned out that getting on the plane was the easy part. When we arrived at her seat, as you might guess, someone was sitting in her child's seat. The attendant was summoned, and a rather lengthy negotiation began because the plane was overbooked. All the time, the three of us, children in hand and carry-on luggage strapped around our necks, blocked the aisle as we waited for the issue to be settled.

Eventually the seating dilemma was resolved and the young family settled in their seats. Unfortunately, by the time they were seated, all of the overhead compartments were filled and there was no place for the young mother's five carry-on pieces. The attendant huffily gathered the extra bags and began a search for empty space. When the plane finally took off, the five bags were spread over a twenty-row area.

The flight itself was equally disastrous. The infant cried the whole five hours we were in the air and soiled his diapers several times, requiring a diaper bag's retrieval each time. The two-year-old proved himself to be a major leaguer in terms of hyperactivity.

By the time we arrived at our destination, hours later, the young mother was frayed at the seams and near tears. Most of the seatmates surrounding her were involved, if only because they were irritated. The airline attendants, who helped as much as they could during the flight, smiled collectively as she deplaned. Their ordeal was over.

I'm sure the young mother and her children suffered the most.

If I were she, I would have ended my trip vowing not to fly again until my children were of college age!

The young mother is a lot like those of us who want to love God. We naively believe that the journey will be simple and uncomplicated. We just want to sit back and enjoy the trip. But alas, that's just not possible.

All that complicated her journey, her two children and her five extra pieces of baggage, represent the multiple issues we frequently take along on our journey—the issues we will discuss in this book. The attendants and the passengers are our fellow life travelers who can make our journey easier, but more often than not make it more difficult.

In the same way that the young mother couldn't possibly enjoy her first trip in an airplane because of her overwhelming situation, those of us who carry unresolved personal and relational baggage can't possibly expect to enjoy our journey with God. The romantic idealism of the travel brochures is clouded over by the realities of our trip.

Hurt, fear and defensiveness collect like cameras around the neck of a tourist. Broken relationships tug at our memories. The purpose of this book is to unpack this baggage and ask ourselves if it's absolutely necessary to take each piece along. What we don't need we'll leave behind. When we must take something with us, we'll know why we're doing so.

A Moment of Truth

I invite you on this journey because I've traveled the first leg myself and have come to know the self-searching process well. Though I've been a Christian for well over twenty years, it was only a number of years ago that I realized I'd exceeded my excess-baggage limit when it came to my relationship with God.

I was studying the context of the Lord's Prayer in Matthew 6 to teach a Sunday-school class. As I read along, I realized that Jesus' words about the Pharisees were uncomfortably true of me as well. Most of us don't mind seeing ourselves in the disciples. They had their failings, but their hearts were in the right place. The Pharisees, however, were the number-one hypocritical religious leaders of Jesus' day. They spent more time trying to look and appear religious than they did in trying to love God and others. Who would want to identify with them?

Fortunately Jesus' words confronted me at an honest moment. What followed was a time of painful self-evaluation and reflection. If I wanted to identify with the disciples, not the Pharisees, I would have to change. Acknowledging this was hard for me to do, but it was good at the same time.

During my struggles with Jesus' prayer, I had a discussion with a friend who was wrestling with the same issues. Frankly, her pain was greater; where I was experiencing discomfort, she was experiencing despair. Her marriage was in tatters; her children were rebelling; and she was understandably depressed.

But she felt the greatest pain over what she saw as her own spiritual failure. Her anger, turned in on herself, had become depression. She had tried the traditional spiritual disciplines, and they had not seemed to work. She had tried the summer-Bible-camp approach she had heard as a teen: "You can't possibly be spiritual so don't try. Leave the work to Jesus and relax." She *had* left the work of being spiritual to Jesus and it still wasn't working. Neither had any other spiritual formula that had come her way.

Both of us had experienced conversion, she at age ten and I as a seventeen-year-old. She had been raised in the church, and I had been active in church since my teen-age years. At the time we talked about loving God, we each had been Christians for more than three decades. By any stretch of the imagination, we were veterans. And yet, we both were struggling with our faith.

As we talked, it became clear to me that developmental and psychological issues were affecting our ability to love God, just as they affected our ability to love the other people in our lives. In that sense, we were brother and sister hatched in the same nest!

In my twenty-five years as a therapist, I have interacted with thousands of genuinely committed Christian people about their relationships with others. I've come to believe that not everyone has an equal ability either to love or to receive love, whether or not they are committed Christians. Much personal history intervenes. A person's ability to love is influenced, if not determined, by the person's psychological and relational history. If this is true in terms of our human relationships, why wouldn't it be true in terms of our relationship with God?

To me, this is the key issue of spirituality, but in a very specific sense. For some, spirituality has to do with memorizing Scripture, reading the Bible and praying daily—the spiritual disciplines. For others, it may involve the daily witness about faith in Jesus Christ as Lord. And to still others spirituality means an inward attitude of quiet reverence or self-sacrificial service to those around them. I define *spirituality* as "loving God." And when I talk about loving God, I mean the same kind of passionate, committed or self-sacrificial love we can feel and demonstrate toward anyone else—whether a spouse, a child or a friend. We have cause to love God because of who he is and because of what he has done for us, and he expects our love.

As I cut through the complexity attached to the issue of spirituality, loving God became the central issue. But loving God, as in loving anyone, is harder than I had been willing to admit. Beneath the simplicity lies the complex issues involved in loving anyone.

No matter how difficult loving is, I've concluded that it's impossible to say you love God while at the same time you hate your neighbor, act unkindly or abusively toward your family, or treat your own personhood with disregard or disrespect. Loving God begins with the capacity to love, period. Certainly not with the capacity to mask failures and inconsistencies and to pretend and hide.

This realization seemed to be a key to my struggles with the Lord's Prayer and my hypocrisy. It also led to discovering a root cause of my difficulties. Maybe the source of my hypocrisy lay not in my spiritual being but in my psychological self. I had never looked at that part of myself in terms of my relationship with God—though I had, of course, in terms of my relationship with my wife and my children, and had come to some very powerful, life-changing conclusions. I realized that a missing aspect in the traditional discussions about spirituality is how our ability to love others affects our ability to love God. The process is a two-way street. I needed to apply what I knew about myself developmentally and psychologically to my relationship with the Father.

When Jesus taught his disciples to pray, he probably made some assumptions about their emotional development, their psychological makeup and their cultural perceptions. We know a lot more about those areas than was known in the first century; however, we can assume that when Jesus instructed his disciples regarding their walk with God, he knew both the simplicity and the complexity of their personalities and their surroundings. He understood the dilemmas they faced as well as their temptations. Although the *categories* of human development, psychology and culture were not in use in his day in the same way they are today, the *meanings* beneath the categories were.

Jesus understood his disciples in the same way he understands us. That's not the question. The question is, do we understand him and what he asks of us enough to love him as he loves us?

And if we're struggling with loving him, what's getting in our way?

I'd like to take you on that same journey of self-understanding I've experienced by making the Lord's Prayer a mirror of our lives. As we study the prayer phrase by phrase, try to evaluate your spirituality in light of the prayer. Of course, there are comparable Scripture passages that would allow us to evaluate how we love God; I chose to focus on the Lord's Prayer because of its unquestioned importance to the worship experiences of the people of God.

In studying the prayer, we will address the following questions:
☐ In order to pray the prayer as Jesus intended it to be prayed, what is assumed about those who pray it?
☐ What kind of "lovers" are they?
☐ What are the issues that undergird the prayer?
☐ How do those issues affect our ability to love God in the way we believe we ought to love him?

For some of us, the issues that come up will be as simple and straightforward as the prayer is easy to summon to mind. For others, the issues may not be so simple, straightforward and easy to grasp. It is for those of us for whom loving God is not always so easy that this book is written, and it is to those same people it is dedicated.

CHAPTER TWO

WHEN WE'RE NOT WHAT WE PRETEND TO BE

I f *this is a book about loving God, then this is a chapter* about pretending we do when we don't. Pretense is a part of human nature. We all want to appear to be better than we are.

Suppose, for example, it's Valentine's Day. I might have a few extra dollars in my wallet put away for a fishing rod I have my eye on. As I drive home from work I pass the corner florist. He's displaying bouquets of flowers outside his shop. I catch a glimpse of them as I drive by. My instincts tell me that my wife would appreciate some flowers to commemorate the day. Instead, I pass the florist's shop without even a shift in gears.

At home, the evening meal is unusually festive. As the meal is served I pretend not to notice the specially prepared food, the attractive table settings and the candlelight. When the meal is finished, my wife looks disappointingly at me as if to say, "You forgot, didn't you?"

I fake a question: "What's the matter?" She responds testily about not feeling important to me anymore. I respond defensively about all the "loving" things I do that she never acknowledges. The dinner ends in silence. I mutter under my breath that Valentine's Day was created by a bunch of money-grubbing card, candy and flower merchants and that I'm right to ignore it all.

Here's a related problem. Let's suppose that last Sunday in church the pastor preached a sermon on husbands loving their wives as Christ loved the church. I listened and nodded at the appropriate times. I even commended him for his message as we shook hands at the door. Unbeknownst to anyone, his words had run off my soul like water off a duck's back. I didn't hear a thing. For all intents and purposes he was preaching to someone else.

According to my Valentine's Day story, in the same way I ignored the pastor's sermon, I ignored the issue of my wife's feelings and the consequences of my choice to save my money for the fishing rod rather than spending some on flowers for my wife. (I've learned that if you ignore an issue long enough, it will go away, even if it's important to someone else.)

We can respond similarly about the issue of loving God. We can pretend that the sermons and the questions are for someone else. They don't apply to us because we've already decided that we love God even if the tangible, demonstrable measures of our relationship indicate otherwise. If we ignore the pressure and the discomfort long enough, it will just go away as always.

Do I love my wife? I say I do. I can even make it appear as if I do. But don't ask me. Ask her! She knows for sure. And she knows whether my "love" for God makes any difference in the way I live and treat others, especially those closest to me.

Sometimes it's both embarrassing and painful to look at ourselves full in the mirror of our relationships with others. The cosmetic of self-deception, useful to cover our flaws from ourselves, is useless when we look at ourselves as others experience us. That's the key: to see ourselves as others see us and not necessarily as we want to see ourselves nor as we want others to see us.

Such was the case at the time Jesus taught his disciples to pray what we refer to as the Lord's Prayer. The passage of Scripture that wraps around the Lord's Prayer like ribbon around a package, the Sermon on the Mount, contrasts the differences between those who are concerned with how religious they appear and those who are genuinely religious. The Pharisees were mostly concerned with their outer selves. Jesus taught his disciples to be concerned with their inner beings. Loving God begins where the context of the prayer begins: an honest appraisal of who we really are before God.

How We Face the Issue

In evaluating our relationship with God, we have several options in handling unwelcome information about ourselves.

☐ *Ignore the problem.* The most common response to unwelcome information about ourselves is ignoring it. The Valentine's Day situation is a good example. When it comes to spiritual issues, it's very easy to live as if negative or critical information about relating with God best applies to someone else and not us.

☐ *Rationalize it.* Another option when faced with our hypocrisy before God is to explain it all away. We play games with words like *loving God* and *spirituality,* defining them in whatever way fits our predispositions. We escape through the vagueness of our definition and thus obscure the distinction between those who love God and those who don't, the distinction Jesus makes in the

Sermon on the Mount between the hypocrites and the disciples.

If we're quiet by nature, we can define spirituality as a "quietness of spirit." Or if we're in the habit of attending church regularly, we can make spirituality out to be faithfulness in the support of church programs. Loving God becomes whatever we rationalize it to be, and we let ourselves off the hook.

☐ *Intellectualize the issue.* Or perhaps we can make it a game—a kind of religious Trivial Pursuit. We can analyze it, debate about it, write books about it, preach about it and memorize Scripture passages about it. We treat the issue of loving God as subject matter to be studied and discussed. After we've theorized about the minutia of the matter, we live as we did before, without allowing the words we have studied to confront us. They remain words on the page of a book or words spoken from the pulpit and not the word of Christ for us.

☐ *Face the issue head-on.* Last, we can face the issues squarely and realize that when it comes to an honest definition of *spirituality,* we all are more like the hypocrites described in the Sermon on the Mount than we'd like to admit. We can figure out why that may be so and then do something about it.

A Public and Private Reality

The last option, the one most of us would like to believe we would choose, is more difficult than it appears on the surface. What makes it difficult?

Matthew 6 includes Jesus' lengthy analysis of the Pharisees' religious motivations. According to Jesus, they were religious in the sterile sense of the word. The forms of their religion had taken precedence over the reality. They "appeared" to be on the outside what they weren't on the inside. Their concern about appearances made them hypocrites. They were practicing what I refer to as "mere religion."

The context of the Lord's Prayer is a kind of spiritual test, measuring the degree we have or have not been infected by the hypocritical virus of "mere religion." The questions to ask yourself are the questions I asked myself: "Just how much of a hypocrite am I?" and "If I am, what can I do about it?"

Mere Religion

In the Sermon on the Mount Jesus said, "Be careful not to do your acts of righteousness before men, to be seen by them. If you do, you will have no reward from your Father in heaven" (Mt 6:1).

The first test of the "mere religion" virus is *whether or not your acts of love become means to personal ends rather than ends in and of themselves.*

I'm familiar with an incident that involved a national Christian television broadcast and a small, Christian mental-health agency. The small Christian agency was being sued by an organization over a situation that involved constitutional issues having to do with freedom of religion. The agency's strategy for raising funds to pay for their very expensive lawsuit included an appearance on a national Christian network. When the day arrived, the executive director of the agency was interviewed on camera by the televangelist host.

The director of the agency told his story, and the host turned to the video audience and said something to this effect: "This is a terrible breach of justice. It ought not to be allowed to happen in America. It's exactly why you need to support our broadcast. So that people like our friend here will have a place to tell their story." In other words he said, "Pray for them, but give to us."

The story's sequel came two or three months later, when the executive director of the agency learned from someone on the televangelist's staff that several thousand dollars in contributions for the network were raised as a result of that particular program.

In contrast, the agency being sued received less than one hundred dollars in gifts toward the expenses of the lawsuit.

It's not my point to bash televangelists (they have enough problems these days). What occurred that day illustrates the hypocrisy of "mere religion." Hypocrisy reverses means and ends.

The financial need of the smaller agency was a legitimate end in and of itself. The financial need of the Christian television network was a legitimate end as well. "Mere religion" occurred when the televangelist ignored the legitimate need of the smaller agency and used their plight as a means to his own ends while leaving the impression that he was being compassionate and loving. When we use the plight of others for our own ends, we are hypocrites.

To be honest I can't throw stones at the televangelist. Why? Because I'm reminded of an occasion when I gave less money than I normally would have to a needy person because I couldn't claim my donation as a charitable gift for income-tax purposes. As far as I can tell, the only difference between the televangelist and me would be the level of public notoriety. Hypocrisy, like the virus of the common cold, is easy to catch and sometimes hard to get rid of.

The second test for "mere religion" comes from Jesus' words when he said, "And when you pray, do not be like the hypocrites, for they love to pray standing in the synagogues and on the street corners to be seen by men" (Mt 6:5). *Loving God is mere religion when prayer becomes an act of public pride more than an act of private devotion and petition* (see Mt 6:5-6).

The Pharisees, the hypocrites in the Sermon on the Mount, enjoyed playing to the crowd. They were exhibitionists—human peacocks spreading their feathers for everyone to see and then preening when others looked. They did it all under the guise of prayer.

Jesus condemned the public display of religion when that display isn't backed up by private behavior. According to Jesus, the hypocrites got just what they wanted: the attention and approval of people but not the attention and approval of God. Their prayers were empty, devoid of power.

I often wonder how our public prayers that sound so good to us are received by the One to whom they are addressed. What does God think of how we pray?

In an upside-down kind of way, a story about a young associate pastor in a large church illustrates my point. Upon walking onto the platform of the church one Sunday morning, he discovered that he was to offer the prayer of confession in the service and he hadn't thought out nor rehearsed his prayer.

When the time came, he began to pray, and without thinking he blurted out in the context of his prayer that he needed the Lord's forgiveness because the night before, while angry with his wife, he had smashed his fist through a wall and his relationship with her was strained to the breaking point. He sat down to the absolute silence of the congregation, including the senior pastor who should have followed him in the order of service. Everyone was stunned.

Upon sitting down, he realized what he had said. He didn't hear another word for the rest of the service, he was so embarrassed and desperate to get away. The sermon, the hymns and the benediction were lost in the haze of his humiliation.

At the end of the service, when every part of him wanted to run, a peculiar thing happened. Person after person approached him and thanked him for his honesty. Some confessed similar struggles to him. They all committed themselves to pray for him and for his wife.

His prayer did create controversy, however. Later, some of the elders of the church questioned the appropriateness of his confession. They felt that it had diluted his effectiveness and had tarnished his image. Even so, the dialog that followed between the pastoral staff and the lay leadership of the church was a step forward for the entire church.

Just how real ought we to be when we pray in public? Admittedly there is a fine line between exhibitionism and public contrition, but who can know? Probably only the one who prays. Somehow, I believe that during that Sunday morning service God was moved by the young pastor's prayer. Whatever happened that morning was not "mere religion."

The third test for "mere religion" centers upon the New Testament practice of fasting. In Jesus' day people dieted for religious purposes more than they did in order to lose weight.

Jesus said, "When you fast, do not look somber as the hypocrites do, for they disfigure their faces to show men they are fasting. I tell you the truth, they have received their reward in full" (Mt 6:16).

"Mere religion" is *when personal discipline is overshadowed by public notoriety.* Whatever fasting meant at the time, Jesus' concern seemed to involve the Pharisees' practice of wanting to look like they were religious when they weren't.

An article in our local newspaper described the avant-garde exercise boutiques of Los Angeles. The writer couldn't help but notice how important it was to the exercisers to "look" the part. That meant having the right pair of shorts or tights, a particular kind of running shoes, color-coordinated outfits designed to communicate that the wearer was serious about his or her physical self. If you didn't look the part, you couldn't fit in, no matter how in shape you were.

The fourth and final test for the hypocritical virus of "mere religion" has to do with priorities and ultimate values.

Jesus said, "Therefore I tell you, do not worry about your life, what you will eat or drink; or about your body, what you will wear. Is not life more important than food, and the body more important than clothes?" (Mt 6:25).

This is the test that gets most of us: *Loving God is mere religion when our worries about today displace ultimate values.*

Jesus, in the Sermon on the Mount, focused the disciples' attention on the rigorous demands of the kingdom of God. Nothing and no one was to come before it. His was a radical cause accompanied by radical demands. His demands were such that earnest people like the rich young ruler turned away from following him because it would cost them too much.

Christianity was never intended to be a comfortable religion.

Jesus focused upon very ordinary ideas and behaviors. He talked about what we eat, what we drink and how we clothe ourselves. He talked about the ordinary dimensions of our lives, all of which can be good in and of themselves. Later in the Gospels he would talk about husbands, wives, children and parents. "Present concerns" involve anything and anybody that have the potential of placing ultimate demands upon our loyalties.

The virus of "mere religion" replaces Jesus with whatever appears to be good for whatever reason.

Said in another way, whatever dominates the horizon of our lives other than Jesus Christ as Lord is an idol. Whatever we focus upon to the exclusion of everything else has become an idol. A man who is a workaholic is an idolater. So is the young woman who drives herself to succeed in school to the exclusion of all else. As is the mother whose anxieties about her children chain her and them to their home.

Idolatry involves replacing the person of Christ with the presence of anyone or anything else.

Jesus said we are to "seek first the kingdom of God" and all else would fall into place. In the case of this fourth test for "mere religion," it is our relationship with Jesus Christ and his kingdom that keeps us on course.

An Honest Response

Loving God begins with an honest evaluation of our faith.

Loving God sometimes begins with the prayer of the tax collector in the Temple, "God, have mercy on me, a sinner" (Lk 18:13). It begins with our being honest with ourselves and others as well as with God.

The kind of honesty I'm talking about was illustrated by a clergy family I worked with in therapy. They had come for therapy because of a teen-aged son's drug-related behavior. The mother, who had initiated the therapy, wanted me to focus on her son, to "fix" him. But, as is my custom, I asked that the whole family come in at least for the initial interview. During the session the anger in the family quickly boiled to the surface in the form of invective which the son poured out on the pastor/father.

The family was sharing their views about "the problem" when the son erupted like Mt. Vesuvius. He screamed at his father for his hypocrisy. How could the father pray such beautiful prayers from the pulpit only to return home to curse his family in private? How could the father act so compassionately in public and forget his daughter's birthday the week before?

Following the son's outburst, the room was absolutely quiet. The mother began to weep. The siblings squirmed in their chairs. The father returned his son's indictment with a silent stare. The secret was out. The son had said he was a hypocrite.

At first the father smoothly countered his son with what appeared to be a kind of client-centered response learned in his pastoral counseling classes years before. He was good. But the son wouldn't let up. We had come to a fork in the road in terms of what the father would do with his son's accusations and anger.

To his credit, the father chose not to return blame for blame. He did not become defensive. Quite the opposite. Though at first he stumbled and stammered, he admitted to the son and to his family that he had been inconsistent. He owned his hypocrisy. It was the beginning of a long and arduous road toward reconciliation.

Eventually, the son, like his father, owned his hypocrisy: He had played the truant, marijuana-smoking rebel, when in his gut he wanted to be loved and accepted by his father. After many tears and more anger the family was able to work through their problems.

For me, the story illustrates the terror of being a servant for Christ in the public arena. It's as if hypocrisy has been institutionalized into the very roles themselves.

We are all vulnerable to accusations similar to that of the pastor's son, if only as a matter of degree. Perhaps the answer to our dilemma lies in the paradox of freeing ourselves from the burden of our hypocrisy by acknowledging that we are hypocrites while at the same time not excusing ourselves because we are.

Remember, God is less impressed by the doing of religious rituals than he is by the intent that lies behind the doing of them. We need to remember that God looks on the heart and man looks on the outward appearance. Sometimes it's hard to love God because it's easier to appear to be "merely religious" than it is to be genuine.

Inevitable Conclusions

It's hard to look at ourselves and even harder to see ourselves as others see us. Before you give up because you've decided it's useless, let me make some suggestions of where we are, so that we can determine in which direction to go.

☐ *We are all hypocrites under the skin, so don't pretend other-*

wise. The pastor/father with his family came to realize this principle very quickly, and his family benefited accordingly. It is best to admit what we're like and not to try to fool others. Everyone else probably knows anyway.

□ *Loving God seems simple at first glance, but it is infinitely complex*. The whole reason for this book is tied up in this principle. Matters of spirituality, or loving God, involve our whole selves and not just our spiritual selves.

However, most of what has been written about spirituality hasn't dealt with the other dimensions of our selves such as our family history, our personalities, etc. This book is intended to provoke us to think about these other issues as well.

□ *We are ultimately accountable for what we do more than what we ought to do*. Beneath this issue is the tension between the real and the ideal, between the here and now and the there and then. What good is it to put forth a spiritual ideal that is inaccessible for most people? I'd much rather start where people are and have them begin their journey from there, trusting in a loving and sovereign God to guide them on the way.

□ *When we fail we have an advocate, Jesus, the Son of God, who understands our dilemma and who will shoulder our burden—both with us and for us*. This truth makes me picture the condemned and beaten Jesus struggling to carry his cross up the hill to his own death (see Lk 23:26). Though his gruesome task is only half over, he is at the end of his strength. Another is asked to step forward to carry what he could not carry, a cross that will bring the convict death.

Jesus knows what it is to carry a burden that is heavier than can be humanly borne. He knows what it is to suffer because of that burden and to be despised and rejected because of it. Whatever our hypocrisy seeks to deny, hide or screen from the sight of others has been experienced by the One who calls us to follow him. He has walked where he asks us to walk, and he has carried what he asks us to carry. In spite of it all, he managed to love his father who asked him to bear it all. Evidently, it can be done.

The virus of "mere religion," the practice of religious rituals and appearances, leads not to loving God but to hypocrisy. Whatever it means to "love God," Jesus knows. I'm sure he knows also that sometimes it can be very hard indeed.

CHAPTER THREE

WHEN OUR UNDERSTANDING OF GOD IS STILL THAT OF A CHILD

*O*ur Father . . ."
How do you know that your view of God is accurate? Do you see him as strong or weak? mean or loving? approachable or hard to find? Sometimes loving God is hard because our understanding of God is unduly childlike. Our perceptions of God can freeze in time if we use the verse, ". . . unless you change and become like little children, you will never enter the kingdom of heaven" (Mt 18:3) to justify thinking of God the way we thought of him in grade school. This confuses *trusting God* with *understanding him*. It means that though our bodies and minds have matured, our expectations of God are out of step with the rest of our lives.

Because our perceptions of the world are so closely linked

with our first impressions, to mature in our understanding of God we first need to understand our parents' view of the world and our experience of their world view and of them when we were children.

Through the Eyes of Our Parents

Imagine yourself living in a newborn's body. How would you describe your existence? Research into infant development would answer it with one phrase: mostly Mom. Studies have determined that babies can recognize the voices of their mothers (or primary caregivers) as early as four to five days old. In four to five weeks, infants can recognize their mothers' faces and begin to respond to their mothers' facial expressions and general attitudes.

Our first view of the world is through our mother's eyes and experiences. Though we receive messages from the world through our own senses, our mothers interpret those messages through their reactions to those situations. These first experiences affect our subsequent experiences with the caregivers who come later—including God. Thus, in terms of our understanding of God, an initial question to ask ourselves is: "What kind of world did our parents create for us as children, and how did they perceive their world at the time?"

Our Parents' World

Many parents communicate a sense of security and well-being to their children which allows those children to grow into mature, healthy adults able to return God's love. Unfortunately, not all parent-child relationships have this happy result. Without intending to, parents can communicate negative messages which indirectly hinder their children from having a healthy relationship with God.

Some parents experience the world as an overwhelming place. Life is just "too much." One woman's earliest memories of her mother were of her mom lying in bed with the drapes closed and the door shut. The mother wasn't sick; she just couldn't cope. The little girl would sneak into her mother's room in the afternoon and lie down on the rug beside her parents' bed to take her nap. She wanted to be close to her mother and this was the only way it could happen.

Later, as an adult, the woman struggled with her own ability to cope with the demands of her world. She often felt out of control or in need of getting others to take care of her the way her mother, in adulthood, had gotten others to care for her.

The woman grew up to share her mother's view of God: God was there to take care of her. When he didn't, both women were compliant but resentful. They resisted becoming adults and responsible for their own care as well as for the care of others.

Other parents experience the world as an evil place. They can barely imagine releasing their children into the real world because of the sin and danger it holds. Sometimes they use home schooling or private Christian schools to shield their children or keep them in sterilized environments.

Later, the overprotected children-now-adults sometimes find themselves struggling with a free-floating inner anxiety. On the surface it seems based on their view of the world as an evil, fearful place. Under the surface, however, they often suffer doubts about their ability to cope with their difficulties. Having been protected from a fearful world, they never developed their own sense of personal strength. Their anxiety can be overwhelming.

Naturally, they want God to be their strong protector. Hearing about violence, disaster and disease in the world, they want to retreat into a God-shaped womb and have him cope with all of it for them. When they can't and the accidents or illnesses of life come close to home, they become immobilized. Why doesn't God come and save them from a world that is so hard, so terrible, so ugly? Where is God when he's needed?

Some parents seek to fight their world, which they view as hostile. For them, competition is a way of life, and they hate to lose at anything. They can be ruthless, if necessary, depending on the circumstance. They're winners, and by implication they can't stand losers.

Often their children grow up to experience a relationship with God that resembles a tug-of-war. Life is win or lose, and so is their relationship with God. It can't be win/win; someone has to lose if someone wins. And God always is supposed to win, so where does that leave them?

Still other parents experience the world as a needy place and are out to rescue the world. Everywhere they turn, someone is in need, whether for the gospel, for emotional comfort, or for advice or instruction. These parents would never admit it, but they see themselves as a kind of "second messiah" sent by God. Often their children feel neglected. Someone else or another's need always comes first. A messiah's family usually has to take a back seat.

When it comes to relating to God, these children-become-adults expect to be neglected by him as well. When it comes to answered prayer or receiving love, life seems to be a series of hand-me-downs, with God as chief steward of the missionary barrel. It's very hard to love God if he loves others more than he loves you.

Through the Eyes of a Child

Children tend to experience God in the same way they have experienced their parents because in the beginning *children see their parents as god.* The younger the child, the more godlike the parent. For example, a young child experiences the parent as *omnipotent,* or all-powerful. Dad can do anything. So can Mom. The parents' bigness, tallness and strength translate into an image in the child's mind of persons who dominate the world.

Not only are parents omnipotent, they are also *omnipresent.* To a child, parents are always there. If you're good they notice sometimes, but they're sure to notice if you're bad. Their presence fills the world as much as their power does.

A third *omni* completes the pictures children have of their parents. Parents are *omniscient;* they know everything. In contrast with children's limited abilities to understand the world, their parents' knowledge and experience is unfathomable. They are god.

Besides possessing all these amazing qualities, *parents are perfect.* These very traits make them incapable of making mistakes. Only children make mistakes! Because of this perception, a child's self-image and self-esteem is often distorted. Young children especially believe that if parents can't be wrong, then anything wrong must be the child's fault.

Furthermore, *to a child, experience and learning are concrete.* Those of us who have been parents of young children can attest to this. For example, I remember when our eldest daughter at five asked, "When Jesus comes into your heart, what does he do with the blood?" She took literally our statement that becoming a Christian meant inviting Jesus to come into your heart.

Children acquire the ability to translate their perceptions into symbols around age ten. Until that time they are very concrete. Therefore our earliest experiences of our parents, stored in our minds, are memories that are literal and explicit. If our early relationships were painful, the pain remains inside as a literal and explicit reality even into our adult years. Often we attempt to reinterpret our confusion or pain to ourselves using our adult ability to symbolize or qualify their meaning. But our first child-hood experience of an omnipotent, omnipresent and omniscient authority was coded into our brains as a literal and concrete reality. Our understanding of that reality, if at all, came later.

Another issue that bears on our perception of God as a parent is a *child's perception of life as a game.* To a child, play is serious work. Because through play children work out and practice the rules, the roles and the expectations of being an adult. The nature of play allows them to do so without the risk of failure or em-barrassment. Play, therefore, is very real. It is the anticipation of what adulthood will be like.

If you're a child, you "play" at whatever you expect your life will become. If your play involves traditional sex roles, then you'll probably live your life as an adult following traditional roles for males and females. If your play involves violence and abuse, so likely will your adult world.

In terms of our relationship with God, our first role models were our parents. Rarely do children fantasize about God, be-cause God is too other-worldly or symbolic. Children do, how-ever, fantasize about adults in general, and parents in particular. Parents determine the rules of the "game."

So, God gives children parents and through the eyes of a child, God is like the parent he gave. I believe one reason God gave parents to children was so that they can know what God is like.

Through the Eyes of an Adult

If your understanding and experience of God is still that of a child, I expect it would be difficult at times for you to love him. You can't remain a child and not suffer the inconsistencies and immaturities of a child's experience of the world. We don't have to be stuck there, however. The answer to the struggle is to grow up, to develop an adult view of God.

☐ *Free yourself of being your parent's child.* I'm constantly amazed at how many grown men and women still relate to their mothers and fathers as children and not as adults. Parents, by definition, relate to children. Adults relate to adults. It's possible, you see, to be your mother's daughter without being her child, or your father's son without being his child. As long as you remain a child to your parents, you increase the likelihood that you'll remain childlike. If our relationship with God begins with our parents, then growing up in our relationship with God involves growing up in our relationships with the ones who raised us.

☐ *Recognize the power of your parents' perception of their world, and choose to develop your own.* Though the world may be a fearful and evil place or full of anger and hostility, it can be a hospitable place as well. We need not be limited to the world view of those who raised us. We can choose to see life differently by keeping what we want of their perceptions and laying aside the rest. We need not be caught up in the toxicity of the past. Being Christians, we can explore for ourselves the world in which we live. Becoming adults gives us the boldness to act.

☐ *Let your parents be your parents and let God be God.* There is something very freeing about disconnecting God from the weight of our relationship with our parents. We are free to experience God as "our Father" who is very unlike our parents, if we so choose. A friend once told me that his experience with God at this level was like seeing a rainbow for the first time. Always before he only saw the rain—never the sun. His world almost changed colors, the experience was so vivid.

☐ *Level with him about what you really think and feel.* This is necessary if you're going to be an adult in your relationship with God. It's the nature of children to hide from their parents. It's the nature of adults to risk disclosing what's going on inside their heads and hearts. Because God is perfect doesn't mean that you can't get mad at him. Not only that, he can handle it. He's not an egotistical father waiting to put you down for your opinion. King David in the Old Testament had a marvelous relationship with God. When he was disappointed with God, he told him; when he was angry, he said so (see Pss 60 and 61).

☐ *Expand your repertoire of communication with God to include a full range of human experience.* This suggestion relates to the concrete thinking of children. When as children we thought of God, we tended to think in the concrete terms of rewards and punishments, of pleasing or displeasing him. Children often see their parents as providers, protectors, guides. As adults, they come to see their parents as good companions. Make it a goal to develop a moment-by-moment relationship with God by taking him into your confidence, talking to him candidly, including him in your thinking, writing him letters, singing with him, laughing with him. Spend time with him not because you need to or because you are his servant but because he invites you to become his friend (see Jn 15:12-17).

☐ *Put aside the negative role models of the past and make Jesus your role model instead.* It's amazing to me how our perception of God the Father changes when we discover Jesus as Emmanuel, or "God with us." The Gospels are full of stories of the One who walked among us. He cried. He touched. He loved. He was among us and because he was here, he understands our struggles, our needs and our temptations.

Beginning to see God through the eyes of an adult is a place to begin. When we pray "Our Father . . . ," remember that the One who calls us to prayer, Jesus the Son, is the One who calls us to be his friends.

CHAPTER FOUR

WHEN OUR EARTHLY EXPERIENCES ARE TOO PAINFUL

*W*hich art in heaven . . ."

In the best of all worlds, fathers and mothers love their children, raise them to be responsible adults and do nothing to cause them harm or injury. Stereotypically, fathers are wise and patient; mothers are warm and loving. Fathers provide for their children both materially and spiritually, and mothers bake chocolate-chip cookies and serve them warm from the oven with glasses of cold milk when their children come home from school. The ideal family lives in their three or four bedroom home in the suburbs (comfortable but not pretentious), attend church faithfully on Sundays and midweek, and eat breakfast and evening meals together. They love each other, and they all love God.

This picture of the world has a kind of Victorian amber tint. It's ideal, but is it real?

In the world I'm aware of, fewer that ten per cent of Americans live in such families. Real families love, fight, hate, work, die, forget, fail, succeed, abandon, get sick and care for one another— pretty much simultaneously. They do all this without much thought, and usually with a reasonable explanation for it all. Theirs is an ambivalent world where opposites coexist. The ambivalence pushes the ideal world aside.

It's a changing world. Very little lasts a long time. Sixty to seventy per cent of all children under the age of five will live in a single-parent home before they reach ten. There is more impermanence than there is permanence, more insecurity than security. It's hard to stay married, let alone be happy. It's tough enough to pay your bills on time, let alone save money for the future. There is danger too. People lock their cars and double-dead-bolt their apartment doors. They walk in groups at night. Women hold on tightly to their purses wherever they go.

In this complex, changing and unsettling world, it's easy to be preoccupied with taking care of yourself but hard to figure out how to love yourself in healthy ways, let alone love others and God. Yet in the same way we have created an amber-hued Victorian ideal for our relationships with one another, we have created a similar ideal for our relationship with God. In so doing, we place the ideal beyond the reach of most Christians. Simply stated, loving God takes place in a difficult context: the place where real people live.

Sometimes Distorted by Experience

When we begin the Lord's Prayer with the words "Our Father who art in heaven . . . ," many of us begin with a relationship with our own parents that was less than perfect—sometimes to a small degree and sometimes to a greater degree. In this chapter, we'll look at five kinds of parent/child relationships and try to determine how those relationships would affect a child's later relationship with God.

As I list and describe each type, ask yourself which, if any, of these types may apply to you. When you're finished, sum up your impressions much as you would add a column of numbers with a calculator, and then draw your conclusions accordingly. The final section of the chapter will suggest ways to act on your conclusions.

☐ *The abused child.* Statistics regarding domestic violence in today's world are staggering. They represent the dark side of our culture. Current studies indicate that between twenty and thirty per cent of all women have experienced at least one incident of sexual abuse by the time they are eighteen, usually abuse by a family member or someone close to the family. The percentage of abuse of boys may be as high as one in seven.

The statistics are equally overwhelming for physical and psychological abuse. A conservative estimate would be that thirty per cent of all American families suffer from some form of serious violence or abuse of one or more of their members. If abuse is so pervasive, what effect does it have on our ability to love and to respond to God?

One effect is *fear.* Abused children learn to live with fear based on the actual or threatened violence in their families. Consequently, a child whose parent is to be feared would find it natural to be afraid of God too. I'm not talking about the "fear of God" referred to in Scripture. That fear is a reverential awe and deep respect. This fear comes from believing that the one who is supposed to love you is more likely to hurt you.

A second effect marring the relationship between abused children and God is *anger.* Abused children grow up to experience an angry God; often they are angry people, though they may mask their anger as zeal or "righteous indignation," depression, or blaming a particular person for things that aren't really that person's fault (scapegoating). Whatever form the anger takes, it's really the abuse of the past wrapped in the emotions of the present. Chronically angry people need to ask themselves if they were abused as children.

The third effect is harder to detect. It is a pervasive *lack of trust.* Abused children early on learn to distrust those who claim to have right and pure motives. They learn to be on their guard at all times. As adults, when they attempt to relate to God, it's hard to trust him as well. It's not so much that God is out to get them, but if things are going well he's sure to spoil it for them somehow. These adults may assume God is withholding joy and happiness. They think it's just a matter of time before the roof will cave in.

One abused child-now-adult said, in passing, that God was like the government. They both give with one hand and take away with the other. Though it might appear that God cares, he's really doing his own thing and doesn't care what happens to those of us who live here below. This man's cynicism was the outgrowth of a lifetime of parental abuse and a soul bruised to its core.

☐ *The neglected child.* The obvious form of parental neglect is desertion, most often today a result of substance abuse. Drugs and alcohol lure parents into behaviors children experience as neglect. The parents are off chasing some kind of chemical seductress rather than taking care of the business of being mothers or fathers.

The less obvious neglectful parents are the ones whose neglect seems reasonable. Children whose fathers are successful workaholic businessmen or prominent professionals, latch-key children whose mothers work outside the home to help make ends meet—these children may feel neglected but because it appears that their parents cannot help nor avoid the neglect, these children bury their feelings of neglect, and both the parents and children deny its existence.

An article in a local newspaper about latch-key children is typical of the legion of children affected by this today. In the article, the interviewer reported several conversations with eight- to ten-year-old children who on the one hand defended their working parent(s) because they were away at work, while on the other hand they admitted that they were struggling with loneliness and feeling afraid. They were afraid of life on the streets, but they were bored with life alone at home in front of the TV. According to the article, the likelihood of their doing poorly in school was significantly greater and the likelihood of their getting in trouble with the law was tenfold. However necessary, parental neglect demands a terrible price.

Parental neglect is a fact of life and feelings of neglect are common. Common as well are the characteristics of the neglected child's relationship with God. Neglected children expect to be abandoned. Most of the time their parents are not there when the children need them. However, when it comes to God it's awfully hard to admit to yourself that you expect God to abandon you. Rather than expecting abandonment, neglected children learn not to expect much from God. If you don't set yourself up to be disappointed, you probably won't be. Their relationships with God are more or less lived at arm's length.

A second characteristic involves a kind of pernicious independence on the part of neglected children. If your caregivers won't be there when they're needed, then you've got to learn to take care of yourself.

In terms of relating to God, it doesn't occur to neglected children to check in with God about what they may or may not be doing. Neglected children experience a latch-key relationship with God in which God is doing his own thing and they are off doing their own thing. The God of neglected children is hard to love because he can't be found when he's needed and he can't be depended upon when he *is* found.

☐ *The pampered child.* The opposite of the neglected children are the children who get most, if not all, of what they want. This is the dysfunction of the baby-boom generation. Paradoxically, the parents who indulge their children are often the ones who were neglected in their childhoods; the parental pendulum swings to the other extreme.

The narcissism of the twentieth century, with its me-first-and-me-only attitude, belies the problems faced when pampered children try or are asked to love God. Like the others, they struggle with their relationship with God as well. Many times, their pervasive selfishness gets in the way. It's tough to look out for others when others have always looked out for you. It's easy to love yourself but hard to love God. And even harder to love your neighbor if your neighbor is defined as anyone whose need can be met by your resources. If you're a pampered child, you want to let God take care of your neighbor while you take care of yourself—better yet, let God take care of you both!

This thinking leads to *seething resentment.* Pampered children expect God to take care of them, and he doesn't. Ours is a generation that was promised that "God has a wonderful plan for our lives." When the real-life plan isn't "wonderful," pampered children-now-adults become plagued by resentment. Their temper tantrums may be covered with emotional blankets, such as depression or psychosomatic illness, but they are temper tantrums nevertheless.

Last of all, pampered children experience *lack of self-discipline.* If you have most things done for you, you probably won't learn to do them for yourself. *Self-discipline,* according to my understanding of the term, involves learning to say no to yourself and being willing to live with the pain of that decision. Self-discipline involves delaying gratification, doing without. Pampered children rarely do without anything so they find it easy to say yes to themselves, even if saying yes is hurtful and destructive. The pampered child typically lacks the traditional spiritual disciplines as well, because prayer, fasting, meditation and Bible study all take self-discipline. Their spiritual pilgrimage is paved with good intentions and promises.

☐ *The parentified child.* The fourth kind of parent/child relationship involves the process of "parentification," in which children learn to parent their own parents. This reverses the traditional relationship in which the parent is the caregiver and the child is the care-getter.

Parentification takes many forms. It can involve literal caregiving, in which the child cooks, cleans and looks after the parent. More typically, these children look after their parents' psychological well-being. They feel responsible for their parents' feelings of self-worth and self-esteem. These children must succeed or their parents will feel like failures, because the children's successes define the parents' successes.

As you will learn later in this book, my mother and I agree that I was a parentified child. My father died when I was seven, and I grew up feeling responsible for my mother. Mostly it had to do with making decisions and being successful. As a child I can remember wanting to do well so that my mother would be happy. I gave her something to brag about. She felt good about herself because her son was doing well in school, in sports and other areas. The discussion that immediately follows has been written on the pages of my own experience.

Often, parentified children feel *overly responsible* for their relationship with God. They cut their teeth on being responsible. By learning as children to care for their parents, they become prodigies at caring for others. As a result, parentified children tend as adults to end up in positions of responsibility—in the family, in the church and in life in general. Feeling as if only they can accomplish a task, they end up taking care of God as well, taking responsibility for what only God can do.

Second, parentified children *take themselves too seriously*. When you think about it, taking care of a parent is serious business. These people have been taken seriously by one significant adult most, if not all, of their lives. Naturally, their relationship with God becomes all-business. Earnest, dedicated and easily impressed with their own importance, parentified children have a hard time believing that God, let alone others, can get by without them. Their pleasure is derived from feeling necessary and essential.

And third, parentified children forever *take on more than they can handle*. Accustomed to carrying the weight of others, they become overcommited, classic type-A personalities who keep multiple balls in the air, even to the point of exhaustion. They easily grow weary of their relationship with God. If God is like their parents, he always wants more and rarely notices how much they've already done. Loving God is hard work, not a relationship to be enjoyed.

☐ *The parental child.* The fifth, and final parent/child relationship involves children, usually eldest daughters, who parent their siblings on behalf of their parents. Where parentified children parent their parents, the parental children parent their brothers and sisters on behalf of their parents, usually their mothers.

Parental children tend to be the worker bees of society. Work, work, work; toil, toil, toil. Their value lies in their productivity and usefulness, not so much in their success. Their self-worth tends to be tied to their role as "mother's little helper," and whomever "mother" is depends upon who needs these parental children at the time.

In terms of their relationship with God, the parental children work so hard that they *become fatigued by overresponsibility.* They can't relax; there's always more to do to keep the kingdom going. If a little work will do, a lot of work will do better. Few others work as hard as they do. Rarely do parental children let God do the work while they treasure the meaning of grace. Their life verse is James 2:26: ". . . faith without works is dead." Their patron saint is Martha, the sister of Lazarus. They, like Martha, are put off by frivolity, even implying, if not overtly stating, that only work is good. Play, at best, is useless if not evil. Worship is a mystery because doing rather than being makes sense.

Second, parental children *try too hard.* They are characterized by their intensity. Parental children believe that good things should come to those who try hard and are earnest in their good deeds. The emphasis is upon the *should.* Life is filled with *oughts, shoulds* and *musts.* These people thrive on duty. The value they place on duty frustrates them most about God. Why does God allow the evil person to prosper and the righteous to suffer? Where does justice fit into the equation of grace and mercy? Can't God tell when they are doing the best that they can?

Last of all, parental children are *plagued by anxiety.* Inwardly they feel impotent because in their role as a parental child they bore a responsibility for their siblings that rightfully belonged to their parents. Much of the time they were asked to do things for which they had neither the authority nor the skills to do. Anxiety dogs their every step. They can't relax because if they do they will fail and everyone will know they're frauds.

In terms of their relationship with God, parental children feel inadequate to the task of serving. Because they were expected to carry out their responsibilities even though they felt ill-prepared, when it comes to relying on the power of the Holy Spirit for their strength they feel like charlatans. Parental children wait for God to expose their shortcomings since they know he knows how inadequate they really are.

They work too much; they try too hard; and they must deal constantly with their anxiety. It's no wonder that it's sometimes hard for them to love God.

So What Can Be Done about It?

We've seen five kinds of children growing up in less-than-perfect families, all in their own way trying to figure out how to love God. As you read the descriptions, which pattern did you find you were identifying with the most?

For some of us, depending upon the level of dysfunction of our families, the answer would be "all of the above." For others, the answer is "none of the above." In the case of the latter response, a sixth kind of parent/child relationship exists: the healthy child. Not everyone has been poorly parented. In the case of healthy children, their childhoods are treasures to be invested and multiplied for the sake of the kingdom of God.

I'm also convinced that when many of us add up the columns of our parent/child relationships, we will find that the dysfunction was relatively minor. Our parents weren't perfect, but they were good enough. For those of us fortunate enough to be in this category, loving God is relatively easy.

But others of us are not so fortunate. What are we to do? I'd like to ask you to think through the following suggestions with me. Take them one at a time. Ask yourself if you have or haven't done the work that each requires. If you have, that's great! If you haven't, now is the time to begin.

☐ *Start by facing the facts.* I'm constantly amazed what deep and abiding rationalizations we weave around the parenting we had. Jesus said that the truth will set us free. Primarily he was speaking of the truth of the gospel, but by implication he was speaking of more. The "more" is that those embracing the gospel needn't fear knowing the truth about their relationships but can embrace that truth as well. Admitting to ourselves what really happened to us as children is the necessary place to begin.

☐ *Forgive as much as can be forgiven.* When you face the facts, you may come to understand that you were indeed hurt and injured as a child by those who should have known better. The key to the process is accepting the legitimacy of the hurt before you move on to the act of forgiveness. Even if our parents did the best they could do, sometimes that wasn't good enough. The residue of hurt is present still. That's when forgiveness becomes important. Forgive as much as you can, and move on to the next step.

☐ *Seek the healing of memories.* God does not intend his children to carry the burdens of their hurts forever. He wants them to be healed and released from their bondage. Picture, if you can, the presence of the living Christ coming to you as a child at the time you were hurt and suffering your greatest injury. Hear his voice as he comforts you, and feel his strength as he lifts you up in his arms. Let the risen Christ meet you at the point of your pain.

As you become aware of your pain, if the weight is more than you can bear or the threat of the pain is overwhelming, seek out someone who is trustworthy and wise, and tell that person of your struggle. Pastors or professional counselors are trained to support us at times like these. You don't have to go it alone. Many times God reaches out through the skill and experience of those trained to be people helpers.

☐ *Find a caring community.* The church is meant to be the place where hurting people can find help with their burdens, where we can find relationships and friendships that heal the damage of the past, where the Holy Spirit pours the balm of God's love over the injuries of the wounded and the sick of heart. God asks the church to be the arms of the risen Christ extended to an injured and dying world. Find a community of believers that is doing that, even if you have to look long and hard. Find those people of God who will be the body of Christ for you.

Believe That God Can Be Different

The Lord's Prayer begins with the words *Our Father . . .* and is immediately followed by the qualifying phrase *who art in heaven.* The phrase lets us know that God is qualitatively different from our parents on earth. For some people it is a source of great hope to know that God's parenting is different from their parents' painful attempts.

How is our heavenly Father different from our earthly parents?

☐ *He is generous, rather than withholding.* Perhaps the most famous verse in Scripture is John 3:16: "For God so loved the world that he gave his only begotten son . . ." (KJV). We meet a Father who, because of his love for us, allowed his own Son to be sacrificed in our place. His generosity is immeasurable. No other gift has matched its expense or equaled its value. Because of his generosity toward us, we have been granted the unique status of being "joint heirs" to God's kingdom with his Son through Christ's death.

☐ *He is forgiving, rather than condemning.* The inconsistencies and capriciousness of our earthly fathers and mothers make us vulnerable to feeling condemned, even if we have been forgiven. The Father in heaven, in contrast, is consistent in his stance toward us. He is like the father of the prodigal son who waits at the end of the road, ready to forgive us our sins and welcome us back from our rebellion. His patience with us because of his

48

forgiving nature is beyond human experience and reason. Although he had the right to judge us because of our sin, he forgives us because of the death of his Son on the cross and because of our relationship with the Son as Savior. He is a forgiving Father.

☐ *He is merciful, rather than punitive.* Mercy is the response of one person toward another based not upon what they deserve but upon the character of the person who is responding. Mercy is that quality of the Father by which he commutes our sentence from death to time already served. The Father's mercy releases us from the bondage of sin, not because we deserve to be released but because of his character. He views our willfulness, clumsiness and failures through the eyes of his patience. He treats us with lovingkindness.

☐ *He is helpful rather than hinderful.* The latter word (I made it up) describes a father who demands a task of his child which the child cannot possibly do and who sets a standard that the child cannot possibly meet. Then he teases and takes glee in the unsuccessful attempts of the child to do the impossible. When the child stumbles, this father laughs.

The Father in heaven, instead, is gracious. He puts his shoulder to the weight he has asked us to carry. He provides the means to meet his standards. His grace bears the weight and the responsibility for his demands. When we stumble, as we always do, he never takes delight in our failures. He never "teases."

The Father in heaven is loving, forgiving, merciful and gracious. We cannot see nor experience the Father as he is, because he is shielded from our view by the images of our earthly parents and our past.

He understands the task before us; his task is similar. God chooses to view us differently because of his Son. When he looks upon us, his view is filtered through Jesus' love and obedience. Jesus has met the Father's demanding standards for us. Because of him, we are acceptable. We, too, can choose to view the Father differently because of the Son.

Jesus is the mediator who takes his Father with one hand and you and me with his other and brings us together as the family of God. We who were aliens and strangers are welcomed into the presence of the Father. Jesus witnesses to us that his Father is of a different sort, and he witnesses to his Father that he has died for us. Because of Jesus, the Father from whom we were alienated embraces us with the loving enthusiasm he reserves for his Son. Because the Father and the Son first loved us, we can return their love.

CHAPTER FIVE

WHEN WE HAVE TROUBLE WITH AUTHORITY

*H*allowed be thy name."

Respecting authority, what it means to "hallow" the name of the Father, is central to loving God. Admittedly, I am making a developmental assumption when I say this. I am assuming that people don't easily humble themselves before God if they have never humbled themselves at all. I am also assuming that respecting authority is a learned behavior rather than something we're born with.

Perhaps I'm stressing the need to respect authority because it's been such an issue in my own life. I am the son of a permissive single parent. After my father died when I was seven, my mother moved us to California to be near her family. I didn't realize it at the time but the neighborhood we moved to was, as one of my high-school teachers was to say later, where the "poor white trash" lived. I grew up in a working-class neighborhood mixed with friends and family who were on welfare. We weren't poor but many of our friends were.

My neighborhood and schools had the usual gangs representing the racial and ethnic mix of the place. By the time I was twelve I had learned why gangs were important. Although I had learned to fight in grammar school, the mean times didn't begin until junior high. I was never tough, and my friends weren't either, but we all knew who was and how to avoid them. Mostly I learned to survive by using my head and being a smart aleck. My eighth- through tenth-grade years involved hanging out on street corners with my friends, cigarettes hanging from our mouths, shirt sleeves rolled up, trying to look like we were "bad."

A mark of street kids is their attitude toward authority. In general they learn to rip off anyone in authority if they can and ignore the person if they can't. Couple this outlook with a permissive home environment and you can imagine what my response to authority became. I learned to manipulate it whenever possible and to resist it the rest of the time.

Then came my conversion. As a seventeen-year-old kid who was full of himself, I committed myself to Jesus Christ, but struggled long after with submitting myself to God. As a young adult and on into my middle years I was coming to realize that submitting yourself to God is the easy part; it's the other people in your life who are harder to submit to. You respect God; you don't always respect other people.

This fact didn't strike home with me until I was in my mid thirties. I was in a job that I liked but was working for a boss whom I didn't respect. As one might expect, he and I had angry words one day and I got fired. At first my wrath burned with righteous indignation. How could he do this to me? Then it dawned on me: this situation had happened before, only not to this extent.

The bottom line was my failure to submit to his authority. Anything else on the table between us was dwarfed by the issue of my attitude toward him. Even though he was wrong about what he was saying to me, he was right about how he felt about me because he was right about how I felt about him. Inside I was still the street-smart kid from the harbor area of Los Angeles. Though I had become a Christian almost fifteen years before, I had not dealt with my overall attitude toward authority, and now it was affecting my career, my family and my future.

Fortunately for me, the issue surfaced with sufficient clarity to make my decision path obvious. I had to learn to submit myself to those in authority over me, even if I didn't agree with them and especially if I didn't respect them.

As I write this book it's several years later, and I'm one of the authority figures I used to ignore. Looking back at my life since those earlier years, I can honestly say that my attitudes have changed. The old issues regarding authority don't get in the way of my loving God the way they used to. Though I'm dealing with other spiritual issues now, I know how important authority issues are.

In the Lord's Prayer we tell God we hallow his name. Christ assumed those listening to his model prayer would know what *hallow* means: to respect authority and acknowledge that authority verbally. In order to mean those words, we must humble ourselves before the One to whom we pray, not just respecting him but deferring to him as well. Respect and deference are two sides of the same coin.

The hitch in our respect for spiritual authority has to do with our subtle rebellion—that rebellion during which it's possible to look on the outside as if we're being respectful when inside we're not. The same way we've learned to pray the Lord's Prayer without thinking about it, we can appear to be respectful and deferential to others, including God, without being that way inside. Perhaps the subtlest form of rebellion is to never even consider the issue at all.

Learning to respect authority is obviously central to our ability to function effectively as adults. It's no less central to our ability to love God. The question is, what are dyed-in-the-wool rebels to do? (By my definition rebels are persons whose relationships with authority figures distort or disrupt their relationships with God.) Learning to relate to authority involves a developmental process related to how we come to understand and perceive God. You'll recognize the similarity.

Different Sizes, Different Shapes

☐ *The authority is bigger than we are.* As infants we learn that authority figures are big and we are small. The mere helplessness of the infant lends authority to those who are bigger and older. As children we are dominated by the physical and "psychological size" of others.

Unfortunately, it's possible to get stuck at this level. We can know we're stuck if we still feel "little" inside even when we know we're not. Maybe we feel insignificant or inadequate, or we are easily intimidated. Whatever we feel, we don't feel grown up. Children inside with adult coverings on the outside, we're easily dominated by the authority of others even though no one knows our secret. If God is "big" and punitive and we are small and insignificant, it's reasonable to fear that kind of God and hard to love him.

If you find yourself stuck at this stage of development, the first step in growing up is to *face your fear.* Begin by recognizing that your fear of something or someone is different from the threat they actually represent. Often a fearful person views the world through the eyes of the intimidated child.

When I was a young boy, I would walk home from the elementary school just two blocks down from my house. My problem wasn't the distance; it was the bully who loved to block my path and pick on me. Every day I would try to walk home only to find that he would find me. He would push, poke and tease until I would run off crying and humiliated. The harder I tried to avoid him the more fearful I became. And the more fearful I became, the more he bullied. We were in a vicious cycle.

One day I came home, tears running down my cheeks, to find my grandmother waiting at the door. Grandma Bailie was an Iowa farm woman who had raised a family of nine children, five of them boys. She was full of the practical wisdom that young boys need at times like these.

She listened to my report of the situation and the estimate of my resources. According to my evaluation, the bully and I would enter the army ten years hence with him still pushing and shoving me around. I wasn't just afraid; I had become fearful.

"You're going to have to fight him, Denny."

Her advice was terrifying, and my response was predictable. Didn't she know that he could hurt me and hurt me badly?

"Just make sure that when he's getting his dinner, you get a sandwich. If you do, he'll never fight you again."

My Grandma was saying that I needed to fight both him and my fear. In the long run if I didn't face it, the latter would defeat me. Well, I did fight him, and he did beat me up. I can still remember my yelling and wailing. But not once during the fight did I stop. He "got his dinner," but I "got my sandwich." I survived and, as she predicted, he never picked on me again.

The lesson I learned and carry with me to this day is that it is our fear itself that defeats us and not what we're afraid of. It's our fear that makes us run away to avoid the risk.

Fearfulness is like an emotional ionization process that is free floating. It attaches itself to whatever person or situation happens to be there at the time. Facing your fear involves recognizing that there are two different things to sort out: fearfulness as a state of mind and our fear of a situation. Facing our fear begins with facing our fearfulness.

The second phase in facing our fear requires us to *develop a strategy* for doing so. Fear defeats us when we let it bunch up like a great big wad inside us. Instead, segment your fear into pieces, and then rank order the pieces from the biggest to the smallest.

Start with the smallest and develop a bit-by-bit program to deal with it. Don't try to take all of your fear on all at once. Some fears go away just by facing them. Others require more. Break the fear down into smaller pieces, and begin with the smallest and then move to the larger ones.

The final phase in handling fears is *getting help if necessary.* Some things, like phobias (such as an extreme fear of heights), can't be put aside easily. We need others who are trained in dealing with fear at this level to be with us as we face our fears. At these times getting help is a sign of wisdom, not an indication of weakness. Find someone you can trust who is wise and experienced, and develop a program with that person for facing your fear.

Don't expect to do it on your own. Remember the lesson of the Incarnation: God's grace and mercy often come wrapped in human forms. He gives us the help we need by sending us the helpers we need. Your helpers won't face your fear for you, but they *will* do it with you. In the end the work is yours to do.

☐ *The authority is smaller than we are.* The second stage of development in terms of children's relationships to authority is their growing perception that their parents are small and they are big. Children grow up. They get bigger both physically and psychologically.

This stage of a child's development involves their belief that they can challenge, defy, resist and oppose whatever it is that the authority figure wants or doesn't want. It is the stage of the defiant child—the time of the terrible twos and threes.

From age four to five, children's defiance changes from "no" to "why?" Children begin to assert their independence. They become "big" and the authority figure becomes "small."

In terms of normal, healthy development, it's important that children come to experience a sense of their own emerging potency. On the other hand, it's important that they learn to keep their own emerging power in perspective. Children shouldn't be allowed to become bullies. That is to turn the tables and intimidate those who are to have authority over them. It does children no good to learn that they can bully or boss their parents around and get away with it.

Children who learn to bully their parents reap tragic results in their lives as adults. They learn to use intimidation as a tool in relationships. They expect others to bow to them and to cater to their wishes as their parents did in earlier years.

Likewise, children shouldn't learn to manipulate their parents, a variation of the pattern of intimidation. Manipulative children are often the offspring of child-centered marriages. When children become the center of their parents' world, the world turns inside out. The children are given power over their parents so that they are able to get their parents to do what they want, rather than vice versa.

In the long run, bullying or manipulative children are the ones who lose. They are robbed of the freedom of just being children. Children get their security from knowing they can do childish things, make mistakes or be irresponsible without distorting the parent/child relationship. Under those conditions parents are in charge and in control. The children aren't the authority figures; other people are.

In terms of our relationships with God, you can imagine what happens when people get stuck at this level. The patterns of intimidation or manipulation are counterproductive with God. Those of us who get stuck at this level try to split God off from our other significant relationships and deal with him as if he were unique. We reserve our intimidation or manipulation for others, such as family, fellow workers, employees, etc. We fail to integrate our relationships with God with our relationships with others.

In contrast with intimidation and manipulation, spirituality, according to Jesus, is like a three-legged stool. It involves loving God and loving our neighbor as we love ourselves. Persons who supposedly love themselves while intimidating or manipulating their neighbors will ultimately compromise their relationships with God.

Many of us get stuck at this stage of development because our bullying and manipulation is successful, not as passing incidents but as lifestyles. Our worlds get turned inside out, with us at the center and others orbiting around us. If you think you might be stuck at this stage, what are you to do?

If you're a bully whose lifestyle has become characterized by intimidating others, you probably will find it difficult to hear or accept that you are. You may find yourself getting defensive or irritated reading this section. Most bullies learn to defend their position by rationalizing their behavior and ignoring the messages that they are bullies that come their way.

If you're not a bully but think that you may have learned to manipulate authority figures, the same tendencies occur. Rebels who are manipulators learn to rationalize their behavior and to ignore the negative messages from others.

The first suggestion is to *look honestly at your past relationships* and to accept the possibility that the way you were taught to relate to authority may have been dysfunctional. This process will pierce your defensive shell with the "possibility" of problems. Rebels who are bullies or manipulators often believe, down deep inside, that they are omnipotent or omniscient. To entertain the possibility of dysfunction is to begin the process of dismantling any godlike fantasies they hold.

The second suggestion involves learning to listen. *Learn to hear the words and the messages of those who know you as you really are.* Do the people who know you and love you seem to be afraid of you? Take the risk of asking them what they think, but be prepared to hear what you don't want to hear.

If upon hearing that you may be a bully, be aware that you may attempt to bully the person into taking back the words. If you're a manipulator you may try to talk the person out of it. It's hard to hear the truth. Listen to what the people around you are saying about you, and take what they say to heart.

The third suggestion is probably the toughest of the three. *Develop specific plans to place another's welfare above your own.* In some ways, this suggestion would seem easy. On the other hand, especially for the rebel who is a manipulator, it won't be. Manipulators blithely justify their actions based upon their ability to convince others of their benevolent motives. In reality, if there is nothing in it for them, they would probably not get involved.

The illustration mentioned in chapter two about the televangelist is a case in point. The TV host who defined his needs as the center of the world and brushed aside the needs of the smaller Christian agency is an example of the kind of manipulator I'm talking about. If we were to question the host, I'm sure he would soundly defend his actions. I am suggesting that a true servant would have acted differently.

In contrast, if you think you may be either a bully or a manipulator, a concrete change in your behavior of serving others will go a long way toward rectifying your attitude toward authority. I connect the two because the bully and the manipulator intrinsically expect others to serve them rather than to place themselves in the role of the servant.

If you develop a genuine attitude of service toward others, it will preempt your bullying or manipulating them. It cannot but change your attitude toward those who are in authority over you. It can only help; it can't hurt, so nothing is lost in the trying.

□ *The authority is worse than we are.* The third stage of development in terms of relating to authority involves recognizing that sometimes authority figures are wrong and we are right. This stage involves a recognition on the part of developing children that their parent(s) are sometimes wrong, sometimes inconsistent and sometimes inadequate. In terms of healthy development it happens somewhere between ages ten and twelve.

If you're a child, it's good for your soul to come to the place where you have to forgive your parents for being human instead of always having to ask their forgiveness. At that moment forgiving becomes a two-way street. Forgiveness, like everything else, is developmental. It involves accepting one's own humanity as well as the humanity of others. It involves removing the branch from your own eye rather than the twig in the other person's. It involves facing your own hypocrisy.

In terms of loving God, the hypocrite finds it easier to ask for justice than for mercy. Judging and blaming are given priority over forgiving and accepting responsibility for one's own actions. It's hard to love God when your natural bent is to point fingers, to blame and to judge.

The plan of action to deal with this developmental issue is

probably the most difficult of all: *Learn to submit yourself to authority even if you don't respect the authority figure as a person and don't agree with the person's decisions.*

Sometimes the value of learning to submit to authority transcends the value of being right. Genuine maturity as a whole person comes when we learn to accept others even when they are wrong and we believe we are right. It will mean keeping quiet when you would normally speak up and accepting the judgments or plans of those you would normally resist. Submitting to authority is easy when you agree with the one you are submitting to. In fact, it only really takes on meaning when it involves the latter.

Earlier I admitted that disrespecting authority was a significant problem for me growing up. It eventually involved my getting fired. As is often the case, immediately after I lost my job I was faced with the same issue. I had taken a position teaching in a nearby graduate school. For two years I was faced almost daily with the need to submit myself to those in authority over me. The person to whom I was responsible demanded that I teach a particular course his way rather than the way I would normally have taught it.

In my mind I knew that I was right. I had only recently received my doctorate and was up to date on all the literature related to the course. He had received his degree years before and was out of date.

Second, the whole issue of academic freedom came into play. It was my course, and the norms of teaching in higher education dictated that I be allowed to teach what I saw fit. His insistence that I amend my course to fit his opinions violated my academic freedom.

As I sat in my office seething over what I was being asked to do, the issue of my submitting to authority came to mind. It was the perfect opportunity for me to learn to function differently than

I had always functioned. What was at stake in terms of teaching the course was certainly important. However, the underlying issue of my relationship to authority was of even greater importance. So I decided to organize and teach the course in a way he could accept while holding on to my own integrity as much as I could.

When I walked into his office and told him of my decision he was flabbergasted. He had expected my resistance and was prepared for a wrestling match. But there would be none of that. I simply said that I would submit myself to him, asked for his suggestions, listened and then walked out of his office.

My whole relationship with him changed from that day on. We never got into the pushing and shoving matches that had characterized my earlier relationships. I had to begin someplace with someone I didn't respect in order for the lesson to become real. He never knew it, but he did me a great favor. He helped me face the demon that had crippled me up until that time. He became God's deliverer.

☐ *Authority has been internalized within us.* The fourth and final stage of development involves recognizing that responsibility for our selves rests not with the authority figures but with ourselves. It is the stage of mature, responsible autonomy. If the authority figures are not present, they haven't taken "authority" with them. Normally, it is the lesson of the teen years.

In the Gospels we see Jesus' disciples develop this understanding in terms of their relationship to his authority. When Jesus was physically present, he was the authority. They were like children eager to have him tell them what to do and where to go. Then he left, promising to send the Holy Spirit, who would be with them as their advocate and their comforter. In the interim between his resurrection and the day of Pentecost they were directionless.

In terms of understanding authority, it interests me that when the Holy Spirit came, he came as one who lives within Christ's followers, not as another external authority figure whose physical presence is necessary in order for the work of God to be done. Jesus as Lord became internalized.

The norm became the mystery of the authority of the indwelling Spirit present in the church as the body of Christ. Consequently, the appeal of the apostles in the book of Acts and throughout the Epistles is based upon the need for unity rather than the threat of punishment. The assumption was that they were adults and not children. Even Jesus is pictured in the book of Revelation as standing at the door of a lukewarm church knocking to be let in. If he doesn't have the right to be coercive in that case, who does?

The parallel in terms of human development comes when authority and responsibility are joined together. Children grow into young adults and accept the need to be self-governed. Conscience is internalized. Right and wrong aren't resident in some external source alone. The rule of God is accepted as the rule for and within their own selves. Though God does exist as an external authority, they are to negotiate their paths in life because God is within them. They come full circle when they are ready to be an authority figure for the next generation.

Persons who fail to develop to this level are forever looking for permission from external authorities. They struggle with uncertainty. They become wedged between the right and the wrong, between the good and the bad, between love and hate, never realizing that sometimes choices in real life are not that simple.

Although absolutes exist, much of life takes place between the extremes. Maturity becomes the tolerance for ambiguity and the acceptance of ambivalence.

The Crux of the Matter
Developmentally, the one who is most likely to be able to "hal-

low" the name of the Father is the person who has learned to internalize authority and to live life from that perspective. Respect and deference come from within, not from without. As I have said before, to hallow the name of the Father demands both.

In order to hallow the name of the Father we must learn to bow our knees to others before we bow our head before God. Having learned to submit to others and to internalize that attitude places us in a position to love God. It allows us to approach the throne of God with boldness just as we are encouraged to do, but to do so with humility. We recognize that our relationship with God is a wonderful gift that demands both our respect and our deference. Hence, he is worthy of our love.

CHAPTER SIX

WHEN OUR MINDS ARE CONFUSED

T *hy kingdom come."*
    What in the world is a kingdom? We easily use the word today, but even casual reflection suggests that we have lost the essence of the word's meaning.

Sir Thomas Malory wrote of the kingdom of King Arthur, the knights of the Roundtable and the intrigue of Merlin the Magician. Arthur's kingdom conjures up images of men in armor riding draped horses as they joust for the attention of beautiful princesses. Its religious motifs are captured in Alfred, Lord Tennyson's poem "The Holy Grail." The kingdom of King Arthur offered chivalry and romance in mythic proportions.

Or, in a more contemporary vein, there is the kingdom of Saudi Arabia, which for me conjures up images of powerful sheiks, vast expanses of desert and immense oil-generated riches (deposited safely in Swiss and London banks) supporting extravagant lifestyles.

Of course, every kingdom must have a king or queen in order to exist, and our understanding of kings and queens is colored by the figurative roles of contemporary monarchs, such as the rulers of England and Holland. They are married and buried with celebrity status and great pomp and circumstance, but what do they *do?* What real power do they have? Their power is a referent power, the ability to influence trends rather than make decisions.

There must be more to God's kingdom than this. But what? And how does it affect our daily lives?

While the issues in the previous chapters are psychological and developmental, our difficulties understanding the kingdom of God are more cultural.

In some ways it's presumptuous of me to think that I can divorce myself from my own cultural bias any more than others who have written about the kingdom of God. I won't even try to expound or explain the biblical concept of the kingdom in any particular depth nor with any supposed objectivity. However, I am concerned with our basic question: When we pray the Lord's Prayer, what does it assume about our ability to love God? What in our culture makes the process of loving God more difficult? In this case, what did Jesus mean by the words *kingdom of God?*

Jesus used the phrase *the kingdom of God* to describe the time when he was here and walked among us. He also used it to describe a time, yet in the future, when he will be among us again. According to Jesus, the kingdom of God was "here and now" because he, the King, was present. Wherever Jesus is the kingdom is.

The here-and-now nature of the kingdom of God is what lies beneath the apostle Paul's teaching in his letter to the Romans that "the kingdom of God is not a matter of eating and drinking, but of righteousness, peace and joy in the Holy Spirit" (14:17). No other verse in the New Testament better captures the here-and-now dimension of the kingdom. The presence of Jesus Christ brings righteousness and peace and joy in the Holy Spirit.

A Kingdom of Righteousness

By *righteousness* I take Paul to mean a sense of personal and corporate godliness and holiness. In terms of our contemporary culture few other qualities are less emphasized or less visible. Think about it. When was the last time you heard a sermon or read a book about godliness or holiness? It's probably been a long time. Most books on the subject are more than fifty years old. It's just not a hot topic today.

☐ *Righteousness is both private and public.* Interestingly, however, since the Watergate scandal in Washington, D.C., in the early 1970s, we're very much aware of issues of public righteousness. We're also aware of a contemporary emphasis upon the issues of integrity and morality of public figures such as politicians and televangelists. The publicity, if we're not careful, allows us to focus our attention on the "other guy" and not on ourselves. It's easy to throw stones at those in public life and positions of leadership and not look honestly at matters of righteousness in our own lives.

I was in a meeting of ministers the day after the recent public disclosure of a televangelist's sexual promiscuity. Listening to their discussion of the issues was interesting, to say the least. For the most part the discussion centered on the shame they believed had been heaped on the church because of his actions and confession. They were concerned with damage control within their own ministries—not the damage to the televangelist's ministry nor the damage to the person and family of the televangelist himself. Not once did they agonize with the one who had fallen. Not once did they fall on their knees to repent themselves nor intercede on his behalf.

When faced with a similar situation that pitted private and public morality against one another, Jesus said, "If any one of you is without sin, let him be the first to throw a stone" (see Jn 8:7). The hypocrites Jesus was responding to were condemning of public sin but tolerant of sin (their own) that was private.

In his customary style Jesus confronted the Pharisees and the teachers of the law with their inconsistency. His example gives us much to think about if we think of the kingdom of God as involving *both* a private and a public morality instead of one or the other.

What would Jesus say to us today when we rail on and on about the sins of public figures exposed by the media? Probably, he would confront us as he confronted the hypocrites of his day.

□ *Righteousness is both personal and corporate.* When we do think of the matter of righteousness, most of us think of personal righteousness to the exclusion of corporate righteousness. By corporate righteousness I mean the responsibility we share together for our collective acts.

The 1988 film *The Accused* illustrates corporate unrighteousness. In the film a young woman is raped in a bar by three men. The men are arrested and as a result of plea bargaining between the prosecutor and the defense attorneys, the three men are sentenced to prison not for rape but for reckless endangerment. The sentence carried the same penalty without the sexual connotations.

On hearing of the plea bargain, the young rape victim is incensed. She had been betrayed because the sexual reality of her abuse had been denied. The prosecutor, a woman, accepts the feelings of the victim and comes to believe that there had been a grave injustice done. However, the rapists had already been sentenced and could not be tried again. That would be double jeopardy.

Instead, the woman prosecutor decides to find and try the men in the bar who had witnessed the rape and egged the rapists on. No legal precedents existed for doing so. The resistance from the male legal community was immense. Only the rape victim understood.

In the film, the "observers" were eventually identified, arrested and brought to trial for soliciting an act of violence. Although they had not literally raped the woman themselves, they were found to be as guilty as the actual rapists because they actively encouraged and cheered as the attack took place. They were corporately responsible.

The notion of corporate responsibility has been lost in most evangelical churches because the concept of righteousness has been individualized much as the gospel has been. We may not cheer when an injustice is done, but we may indirectly support the actions of a corporation or government that abuses and victimizes others.

In limiting morality to its personal and private dimensions it becomes easier to rationalize the matter and easier to hide our own sin. The ministers who derided the televangelist for his sin had failed to recognize the corporate responsibility they bore as well.

In contrast, in some churches the order is typically reversed with an emphasis upon corporate responsibility and a lessened emphasis on private responsibility. Such an imbalance toward corporate morality would focus upon issues such as racism and the evils of apartheid to the exclusion of a discussion of personal fidelity. The fault lies in giving attention to one to the exclusion of the other.

It's not possible to pray "thy kingdom come" and not pay attention to the issues of both personal and corporate morality and character. To leave either emphasis out of the equation distorts our perception of the kingdom of God.

A Kingdom of Peace

In his letter to the Romans, Paul added a second dimension to the here-and-now nature of the kingdom. He said that it involves peace. I like to think of peace as involving a lifestyle of gentleness and unity within and between people.

When I think of gentleness, the music of Debussy comes to mind. Or the pastoral quality of Dvorak's *New World Symphony.* There is a softness about the melody and a quietness implied by the harmony. Not much harshness. Very little dissonance.

Whatever peace is, it begins with a peace with God. Peace with God smooths the edges inside our souls. At least that's what it's supposed to do.

You've heard of the proverbial burr under the saddle of the horse. In terms of the idea of peace, the burr under my saddle is the observation that many of us who supposedly have peace with God don't have peace within. How can that be?

☐ *Because we have individualized the gospel.* Whenever we reduce our relationship with God to a personal and individual decision, we do the same thing to peace that we have done to righteousness.

Peace within ourselves cannot be separated from peace between persons. If the one is separated from the other they both suffer. The gospel of Jesus Christ is both a gospel of personal salvation and a gospel of corporate redemption. When we dilute the one, we dilute both.

Scripturally, the gospel of Jesus Christ connects peace "within" a person to peace "between" persons. It was not by accident that the apostle John wrote that if you say you love God and turn around and hate your brother, the likelihood is that you don't really love God (1 Jn 2:9; 4:8-21). We honestly believe, perhaps unconsciously, that we can be at war with one another and still have peace within. The price we pay for this distortion is dear indeed. It eventually empties our peace with God of content and meaning.

☐ *Because we have separated truth from love.* The separation of truth from love is one side of the coin I have come to define as "truthism." Certainly my experience as a therapist has influenced my interpretation of Scripture—especially in this area. The problem of truthism involves two issues. The first is the belief that the pursuit of truth can be divorced from the practice of love.

We too easily believe we can pursue truth at the expense of our love for others. In theological circles there has been a lot of bashing of fellow evangelicals as liberals by those who justify their behavior because they are exposing error and liberating the truth. Whether truth has to do with the issue of the inerrancy of Scripture, or pro-life versus pro-choice abortion, or the exposure of character flaws of televangelists, the attacks of brother and sister against brother and sister have been especially vicious. Every kind of mean-spirited attack has been justified.

Something about the validity of the argument is lost when people and relationships are destroyed in the name of truth. Something is wrong when error is exposed with glee, when reputations are blemished in triumph.

By contrast, the attitude of the father of the prodigal son would be more appropriate. He recognized the error of his son's ways and the sin that was implied. In so doing he was deeply saddened. I'm sure he agonized over his son's sin, his fall into error. Yet, he made the way home clear to his son. Truth was never separated from the hope of reconciliation.

Those who believe they are defending the truth ought always to act in such a way that the path and hope of reconciliation is as clear as is the course of condemnation. For the father of the prodigal son, truth and love were both necessary conditions for reconciliation.

By this reasoning how we treat one another is a valid measure of the content of our faith. Truth and love; light and life. They are as inextricably linked to one another as day and night. You really can't have one without the other.

But what about justice you ask? Will not such an emphasis upon love move us to compromise the truth and void the issue of justice? When do people pay for their sins?

The answer to the issue of justice lies in recognizing God's greater concern for the matter and in answering the question of who has a right to judge. I like the way the apostle Paul dealt with the issue in his letter to the Romans. He asked the question, "Why do you judge your brother? Or why do you look down on your brother?" His answer was that "each of us will give an account of himself to God" (14:10, 12). Paul had every confidence that God could handle his own battles and defend his own turf.

Paul also wrote, and it seems relevant here that,

If it is possible, as far as it depends on you, live at peace with everyone. Do not take revenge, my friends, but leave room for God's wrath, for it is written, "It is mine to avenge; I will repay," says the Lord. (Rom 12:18-19)

Evidently God does not need an avenging angel. Whatever needs to be done he can do himself. The person who acts on behalf of God does so at the risk of error and with the probability of arrogance.

A parallel example from the world of parenting would be the principle of natural consequences. In the same way parents allow consequences to have their sway at times in their children's lives, it is better to step aside and let the natural consequences of falsehood and error be governed by the sovereignty of God than to act on God's behalf and have our own bias and hostility contaminate the process. God is the ultimate judge and he will not be fooled.

□ *Because we confuse facts with truth.* Confusing facts with truth is the other side of the "truthism" coin. The marvelous German scholar/pastor Dietrich Bonhoeffer, in his treatise on theological ethics, first drew this to my attention.

Facts, according to Bonhoeffer, must be filtered through the sieve of love before they become truth. If the filtering doesn't take place, facts remain barren and potentially harmful. Facts, like statistics, can be used to prove anything you want them to prove. Truth, in contrast to facts, takes the situation into account and considers the relational dimension of the equation. People are always more important than information, whatever form that information might take.

Bonhoeffer uses the example of a schoolteacher and a young boy whose father was an alcoholic. The teacher ridiculed the father to the son. To the teacher the father was a useless no-account because of his alcoholism. The truth, however, was that the father treated his son with love and dignity. Whatever were the facts about the father, the truth was that the father loved the son and the son loved the father.

The humiliation the son felt on behalf of the father resulted because the teacher, in reporting certain facts, failed to find the truth. Bonhoeffer asks the question: which was more important— the fact that the father had a drinking problem or the truth that he loved his son?

"Truthism" does what the teacher did. If you can separate truth from love you can separate facts from truth.

Our defense of truth degenerates into truthism when we gather our facts like numbers in the hands of a bookkeeper rather than like numbers in the hands of an accountant. The latter takes the human dimension into consideration, even if the conclusions are hard to hear and accept. Motive and intent are important factors in the situation. They give perspective to the facts.

Truthism does violence to the peace of the here-and-now kingdom of God. It parades its facts devoid of their context and without consideration of how others are hurt or injured in the process. Love is dismissed as sentimentality and facts are trumpeted under the guise of standing against compromise. Demagogues are embraced as crusaders while at the same time the integrity of the gospel is besmirched in the eyes and experience of our critics.

The here-and-now kingdom of God brings peace. It comes wrapped in the quality and character of the peacemakers who carry it. They are blessed by the Father because they insist that facts, whether data or information, be screened for their implications before they are revealed. They insist that love, which covers or bears a multitude of sins, be the final criterion by which truth is measured.

To invoke the coming of the kingdom involves becoming the peacemaker Jesus blessed in his beatitudes. It involves loving God but not at the expense of injury to those who have been created in his image. If there is unavoidable injury, peacemakers, as would the Savior, bear the wounds themselves, trusting that the Father who knows the end from the beginning will sort it all out in the end.

The Kingdom of Joy in the Holy Spirit

The third dimension of the here-and-now kingdom is that of "joy in the Holy Spirit."

Since I've gone out on the limb and defined *righteousness* and *peace,* I'll do the same for *joy.* What I mean by *joy* is the settled contentment that comes to people who, because of their relationships with God, are able to gain God's perspective on life and its circumstances.

My first thought has to do with the preoccupation in our day and age with happiness. Whether it's selling automobiles or lite beer, the media equates feeling good with having things. One would think, if we believe what we see on television, that owning a particular car or wearing a certain brand of perfume produces a sexual experience. The message assumes that we are all looking for the ultimate orgasm. Maybe we are. If we are, we'll look for happiness in whatever we do. Subsequently, if we don't find happiness in what we're doing, we'll get depressed. If we get depressed we'll crank up the volume of our experience another decibel and try again. The treadmill is never ending.

More is good. Bigger is better. On and on and on.

The scriptural idea of contentment is far more compelling to me. Contentment involves a comfortable acceptance of what you cannot change for yourself. Contentment implies a settled state of mind. It is neither conservative (i.e., unwilling to change) nor boring. In my mind it is what results from a life of righteousness and peace.

The apostle Paul wrote to the Philippians that he had "learned to be content" in whatever circumstance he found himself to be in. He knew how to have much and be content. He also knew how to be content with little. His contentment was predicated on the intangibles of his relationship with God and his connectedness with others.

☐ *Joy is a grace-gift from God.* The joy that is ours in the here-and-now kingdom of God is in the realm or sphere of the Holy Spirit. Paul clearly intends to focus our attention on the supernatural. Our joy comes from God.

Our dilemma comes from the habits we have learned. If we are addicted to happiness, we easily become accustomed to feeling good as a result of the presence of various "things." Maybe it's having enough money to do whatever we want. Or it's having the right people around—or not around for that matter. The yuppie bumper sticker "he who dies with the most toys wins" sums it up.

The realm of contentment I'm talking about is a grace-gift from God. What I mean by *grace* is that the gift of joy is undeserved and not a function of our own merit. We can only receive it. We cannot merit it. God gives it. We accept it.

□ *Joy is not dependent on circumstances.* Life for most of us is filled with hills and valleys. There are more rough places than smooth. A realistic view of our world would lead us to conclude that we need help with the suffering in it more than we need help with the good times. For many of us there are more times of feeling bad than there are times of feeling good. Our difficulty comes not from being up but where do we turn when we're down.

The joy I'm talking about comes from the Holy Spirit in the form of a settled contentment, regardless of the circumstances. The Holy Spirit provides an inner compass that orients us toward God in the worst of times. The good times seem to take care of themselves.

As we near the end of this chapter the hymn "It Is Well with My Soul," by Horatio Spafford, comes to mind. The story behind the hymn is what makes it relevant. It is the story of a man who finds joy in the Holy Spirit.

According to the hymn historians, Chicago lawyer Spafford had invested much of his wealth in real estate just before the Chicago Fire of 1871. Just before this, his son had died. To assist D. L. Moody with a European crusade and to give his wife and four daughters a needed rest, he planned a trip to Europe. At the last moment Spafford was forced to remain behind because of business, but his family went ahead on the S.S. *Ville du Havre.* Their ship, struck by another vessel, sank in twelve minutes. When the survivors finally landed in Cardiff, Wales, Mrs. Spafford had to send him a telegram which read, "Saved alone." As soon as possible, Spafford transited the Atlantic to be with his wife. The story goes that the captain of Spafford's ship awakened him when they passed over the site of the previous disaster. Spafford stood at the rail of the deck at the place where his children had died.

His grief was overwhelming. His tears mixed with the sea spray. He returned to his stateroom and at that time experienced the joy I'm talking about. When he returned to his stateroom he penned these words:

When peace, like a river, attendeth my way
When sorrows like sea billows roll—
Whatever my lot, Thou has taught me to say,
It is well, it is well with my soul.

Tho Satan should buffet, tho trials should come,
Let this blest assurance control,
That Christ has regarded my helpless estate,
And hath shed his own blood for my soul.

My sin—O the bliss of this glorious tho't—
My sin, not in part, but the whole,
Is nailed to the cross, and I bear it no more,
Praise the Lord, praise the Lord, O my soul!

And, Lord, haste the day when the faith shall be sight,
The clouds be rolled back as a scroll:

The trump shall resound and the Lord shall descend,
"Even so"—it is well with my soul.

For Spafford, the prayer "thy kingdom come . . ." would be rife with meaning. His ability to declare that it was well with his soul, even in the midst of great personal tragedy, was the mark of a life marked with meaning by the Holy Spirit. As it was for him, so it can be for us.

It is the nature of the human spirit to want to steer around the storms of life, but it is also a reality of life that says we need help to steer through them when they come. It is the nature of storms to get us wet, drenched and waterlogged. Loving God, according to this criterion, is to survive the storm, not to come through dry. Success, according to this measure, is to live through another night or week, to survive rather than die or go crazy.

Joy in the Holy Spirit implies that you can find meaning whatever your circumstances. You can know the love of Christ in the midst of death or life or whatever life brings. Joy in the Holy Spirit is for all the unfair places of life, for all the injustices. It is for all the times we are squeezed dry of hope and find ourselves running on empty. It is for the times we want to quit but can't.

In these times, when we need direction, we need to pray "thy kingdom come. . . ." It is for the times when it is hard to love God.

CHAPTER SEVEN

WHEN OUR LIVES ARE DIRECTIONLESS

*T*hy will be done in earth, as it is in heaven."
If I were to ask most Christians if they "believe" in the
Second Coming of Christ, I'm convinced most would
answer yes. If, on the other hand, I asked, "What difference does it make in the way you live?" most of us would admit
that it makes very little difference at all.

Yet it *does* make a difference—or at least it should. Christ's
planned return to exercise God's will on earth is the reason that
loving God demands living in light of goals. It is the aspect of
loving God we affirm each time we speak the phrase of the Lord's
Prayer, "thy will be done on earth as it is in heaven." Here the
prayer rests on a major teaching of the Old and the New Testa-
ments: One of the Father's goals is that we move toward a day

when Jesus Christ will reign over all creation.

I don't want to start a debate about the end times; that could easily derail our thoughts. I'm more interested in what most Christian scholars agree about: Jesus Christ is coming again, and when he comes he will rule over God's creation, exercising the Father's heavenly will right here on earth.

A Kingdom That Is "Yet to Come"

The yet-to-come kingdom merits serious consideration; it should change the way we are living. Let me use an analogy to illustrate how.

When the 1988 presidential election campaigning began, on the Democratic side of the ticket there were several candidates. They each traded charges and countercharges as the primary campaign progressed. Each candidate had his spate of supporters. Other Democrats remained neutral. As is the case in primaries, one by one the candidates fell by the wayside, and Governor Michael Dukakis from Massachusetts marched to winning the nomination. The groundswell grew, and it became increasingly clear that he would be nominated. Public figure after public figure joined his ranks, endorsing his campaign. Why didn't they wait until the Democratic convention in Atlanta? Because they looked to the future and were able to anticipate his nomination. They wanted to get on the train before it got to the station!

The future thus shaped the present. In terms of the electoral behaviors of the Democrats, Governor Dukakis was "coming," in that he would soon be Presidential Candidate Michael Dukakis. The more certain the result in Atlanta became, the more deliberate and clear the decisions to support him beforehand. Where the Democratic ticket was going determined what the Democrats were doing.

The parallel with the Second Coming of Christ is clear. I'm

certainly not suggesting that Governor Dukakis is messianic and Massachusetts is the New Jerusalem. I *am* suggesting that the future can and should shape our behaviors in the present.

However, this is rarely the case. You're probably asking why. How can such a central doctrine of the church be so impotent in terms of its influence on our behavior?

I believe the doctrine of the Second Coming of Christ affects us so little because of the values in our culture. They make it hard for us to anticipate the future and to understand what's really at stake.

The Centrality of Values

Most of us use the term *value* as if we knew what we were talking about. However, the concept isn't as simple as it first appears. When I use the term I mean that any object, whether material or immaterial, has a value or importance determined by our personal and shared experience of it.

Some objects, such as human life and motherhood, are valuable to us because they are very important to each of us personally as well as to others who share our common culture. Other "objects" may be of neutral importance because we don't care one way or the other about them. For instance, spouses who are baseball widows (or widowers) will be apathetic should the New York Mets clinch their division and play the Los Angeles Dodgers for the National League pennant. (As a Dodgers fan, I can hardly understand this, but there it is.)

Still other "objects" have negative importance and value. They leave a bad taste in our mouths. For many people, genocide or the racism of Adolph Hitler's Third Reich fall in this category.

Values of the Yet-to-Come Kingdom

Because we live where and when we live, we have learned to

value certain things more than others. The key is identifying the things in our lives and what importance we've attached to them. If we want life on earth to be like life in heaven, as we pray in the Lord's Prayer, then we'd better figure out the value we place on those things valued in God's kingdom. We may decide there are things we need to do to align our values with God's.

When I think of the yet-to-come kingdom of God, I think of the *ability to delay gratification.* In a day and age in which immediate gratification is the norm, "getting it all and getting it now" is a lifestyle. After all, "you only go around once in life so go for the gusto."

It's not hyperbole to say that contemporary humanity seems to want it all and to want it now. The pervasive influence of sexual gratification and the pursuit of drug-induced highs are not accidents. They reflect a value system that systematically chooses immediate gratification over the delay of gratification. The need for immediate gratification screens us from the influence and potential of the future, compressing life into the here and now with little thought of the yet to come.

In contrast, the New Testament is filled with exhortations such as a follower of Jesus must "deny himself and take up his cross" (Mt 16:24); Paul says to "put off your old self" (Eph 4:22). Our example is Jesus, the Son of God, "who for the joy set before him, endured the cross . . ." (Heb 12:2).

It may be that we endure so little in the present because we anticipate so little joy in the future. The ability to delay gratification implies the ability to wait, to anticipate, to look beyond the present, to count the cost before you act. It implies thinking about what you're doing before you do it.

While it's true that too often Christians promise "pie in the sky, bye and bye," it's also true that, as Christians, to remove the promise of heaven from our experience of the earth is to remove the perspective that the future provides for the present. It changes our experience of the earth now.

It's important to me as a Christian to know that the present exists in anticipation of the future; life is more than a here-and-now experience. Because of the yet-to-come dimension of the kingdom, the future enriches the texture of today. The values underlying the Lord's Prayer give us the freedom to experience the richness of both.

A second value of the yet-to-come kingdom is the *ability to plan ahead,* to articulate our purpose in life now based upon our understanding of what is yet to come. If there is a relationship between the present and the future, no other facet of human behavior will be more affected than our ability to think in terms of what's coming and to plan accordingly.

Looking back at my life before Christ, probably no other dimension of my life has been changed by the gospel more than my ability to plan for the future. As a boy, my family lived from Friday paycheck to Friday paycheck. As a teen-ager, the first of the week was spent getting over the activities of the previous weekend. The middle of the week was spent anticipating the end of the week, wondering what I was going to do Friday night through Sunday. Life came one week at a time. It was a life without purpose.

In other ways my life was dominated by the present. I received no guidance from home or school as to what classes I should take in preparation for college. No one in my family had gone to college, so no one knew how to prepare. It was all day to day, week to week.

Then I came to Christ. My relationship with God gave me a new vision for the here and now, because I had a vision of what was yet to come. Eternal life became a reality in terms of what I could expect for the future as well as what I could expect from the present. My relationship with God gave me the incentive to plan ahead and the categories around which to organize my future. I learned to plan ahead because there was an emerging sense of purpose in my life.

A third value of the yet-to-come kingdom is the *ability to be goal directed.* A vision for the future acts like a hook and eye to which we can attach the present and by which we can winch the present to higher ground. Thus, the kingdom of God pulls us forward by giving us a tangible goal toward which we can move.

When I was a young man in seminary, my wife and I decided that we were willing to be missionaries if that's what the Lord wanted us to do. We were willing to go wherever we were called. At the same time I was in seminary, I was pursuing a graduate degree in psychology at a nearby university. To make a long story short, God called us to be missionaries but not in the traditional sense of the word. We were called but not to a specific people or place, as might be the case of a missionary to China or Europe. Instead, we felt the Lord's call to be missionaries to the family. We were called to serve an institution rather than a people or a place.

In 1964, when we experienced our call, there were few people we could look to who were missionaries in the same way we were to become. It was much like my experience as a boy when I had no role models to copy and little guidance. But this time things were different and the difference was our ability to factor the principles of the kingdom of God into our decision-making processes, although at the time we didn't really know it.

The part of our "missionary story" that pertains to our discussion about goal directedness is the use Lucy and I have made of that call. We have used it time and time again to guide our decisions about our future. It became the scaffolding within which we built our educational career as well as the litmus paper we used to test decisions about possible jobs, ministry changes and other options.

If I were to cast this example into kingdom language, I would say that our expected contribution to the yet-to-come kingdom helped us to identify both the roles we would play in the present and the plans we would make to prepare ourselves for those roles. What we were to be determined what we were becoming. We used our place in the yet-to-come kingdom as a guide for our choices in the kingdom that is already here.

The Wisdom of the French

I've already said that it's tough to be motivated about whatever we can't experience in the here and now. It's just not our cultural style. Perhaps this is why the Lord's Prayer doesn't focus our whole attention upon some abstract notion of the future. Instead we are enjoined to focus upon the earth as well. The Lord's Prayer involves a real place with real people living in real time. The prayer demands that we integrate the future with the present, heaven and earth, faith and life. Because what we will become has relevance to what we are doing now, the future and present are coequal in importance. We are not to disassociate the one from the other.

The French have a proverb that has always fascinated me. The proverb says, *"You must not only want what you want, you must want what your wants lead to."* In terms of our discussion, if our values are so earthbound that there is no room for heaven, then we're in trouble. It's possible to be so immersed in the world in which we live that we're unable to see and live out God's will on earth.

On the other hand, it's possible to have relegated our faith to such heavenly proportions that it has no earthly link. It is possible to be biblically pure and behaviorally corrupt—to talk the truth and live a lie. None of us wants to think of ourselves as liars. Few of us want to be inconsistent. What can we do to be rid of our inconsistency? Where do we start?

What Must We Do?

I have some suggestions for becoming more consistent.

☐ *Evaluate your goals in terms of what really seems to motivate you.* What are you working for? What do you really want from life? For those of us who are accustomed to living without the thought of goals, these questions are hard.

Now, ask yourself an even harder question: Am I motivated by whatever God's will is for me or am I motivated otherwise? Though it may seem terribly obvious, loving God begins with loving someone other than yourself, or at least in addition to yourself. What aspect of the goals in your life causes you to focus your energies outward toward others or inward toward yourself? One of the toughest issues to overcome is our own selfishness.

Given what I've said, what would you like to do? What contributions would you like to make? What would you like to be remembered for? What do you envision your place in the kingdom to be? Use those answers as a means for strengthening your plans, for reinforcing your resolve. Evaluating the goals in your life is a place to begin.

☐ *Create a purpose statement for yourself that includes the goals you have for yourself and your relationship with God.* A purpose statement is a deliberate exercise designed to answer the questions: Why do I exist? What is my reason for being here? The reasons may be very basic and simple, or they may be sophisticated and complex. The purpose of a purpose statement is to make those reasons explicit rather than implicit, to get the issues out on top of the table. The statement need not be long—just a paragraph or perhaps a page. The idea is to write something down.

Whenever an entrepreneur wants to begin a company or business, the person usually needs to raise money or capital in order to get started. The first step in raising money involves a "business plan"—a set of expectations or goals coupled with reasonable projections as to what the entrepreneur expects in terms of the future. The business plan is designed to be specific in terms of personnel and financial projections but allows for flexibility in terms of day-to-day operations. The prospective investors want to know if their money will be relatively safe. They want to know the risks that are involved. Based upon the information provided by the business plan, the decision is made to fund or not to fund the proposal.

A purpose statement is like a business plan, but the business in this case is our relationship to the kingdom of God. What strikes me as significant is the specificity of our plans about everything in life, in contrast with the lack of specificity about the direction we are moving in terms of God. Typically, we spend more time planning for our vacations than we spend deciding about where we fit in God's kingdom.

☐ *Develop a set of concrete steps you are willing to take over the next few months in order to implement the goals you have for yourself.* The idea here is to begin with action. Loving God doesn't happen in a vacuum. It involves a conscious decision to do something. Do anything, but start somewhere. Maybe one of your goals for yourself involves further study or education. One step might be taking a class in a relevant subject, or beginning a reading program in an area you're interested in. Maybe another goal involves developing self-discipline. You might take the step of beginning a diet or a program of physical exercise. The idea is to get specific. Probably, for most of us, the simple goal of organizing our time to make more time for ourselves and God would be one place to start.

Getting Organized

My hunch is that heaven is an organized place—not slavishly organized, but organized. The acts of the delaying gratification, finding purpose and being directed by goals probably fit there very well. To get these concepts out of the sphere of heaven and into the sphere of earth, we've got to decide to take them seriously.

When you and I pray "Thy will be done on earth as it is in heaven," we can mean it or we can fake it. The decision is ours. That's what makes the earth so unique. The earth holds human beings created in the image of God who have the freedom to love and serve God or to find other goals. In our ability to choose, we're special to God. It also makes the task of loving him very complex indeed.

CHAPTER EIGHT

WHEN WE DON'T KNOW HOW TO ASK

ive . . . this day . . ."

Once on a trip out of town I engaged my seatmate on the plane in conversation. She was an apparently successful but troubled executive on her way to a business convention. We exchanged greetings, and we asked one another what we did for a living. She told me of her position as a sales manager for a large computer software company, and I told her that I taught marriage and family therapy in a theological seminary.

She was interested in what I did until she heard that I was a part of what she called "the religious establishment." As we talked further, it became clear that she had formed a deep distrust of anything religious because she assumed that most, if not all, religion was dominated by and for males.

In all fairness I couldn't deny her perceptions. Most religion *is* dominated by and for males. Our conversation continued about her work, but any discussion about God was over. She talked about her family ever so briefly, and there was a hint of fear mixed with defiance. Her home growing up and her present marriage weren't happy. She didn't believe in God. She would never have prayed the Lord's Prayer because of the situations she had experienced in her earlier religious contexts.

In reflecting upon my encounter, I believe Jesus sympathized with her and her perceptions. He, too, was an outsider in terms of the religious establishment. He, too, was very critical of the religious chauvinism of his day. Eventually, their treatment and hostility toward him led to his death. You can't get more alienated than that!

Had Jesus been the one sitting in my seat, I can't help but believe he would have interpreted God the Father to her more positively than she had experienced him in her previous encounters. The young woman executive would have loved the assertiveness Jesus encouraged when he taught the disciples the Lord's Prayer.

Jesus model prayer is rather impertinent. Taken at face value, it almost invites arrogance, especially when you recall the religious context within which it was given. Remember, at the time Jesus instructed the disciples in the Sermon on the Mount, the Jewish Temple was still in existence. Only the high priest on the holiest of holy days was allowed to enter into the Temple's Holy of Holies. (Did you notice there were four *holies* in that last sentence?) Approaching God was serious stuff!

It was elaborate as well. The rituals of the Old Testament were followed precisely. There were more formulas and instructions for relating to God than the average person could remember.

Whole segments of society, the priests and the Levites, were dedicated to keeping things straight. It was easier to fear God than to love him. It was nearly impossible to be close to him.

Most of all, the young woman in the airplane would have appreciated the way Jesus challenged the power structures of his day. The disciples lived in a highly patriarchal world. The Jewish father, because of his position and because he was a male, was to be revered and obeyed—never questioned. The line of authority was well-defined. Women and children were second-class citizens. Only men were allowed direct access to God; and the older the man, the more influence he had with God and the more authority God bestowed on him. If you were a Jewish child you would have a distant and formal relationship with your father. Most of your close family relationships would have been with women: your mother, sisters, grandmothers, aunts. If you were a boy, you eagerly looked forward to manhood. Girls could only look forward to serving men.

With Boldness and Comfort

Within this context where religion was formal and families were authoritarian, Jesus taught the disciples how to come to the Father in prayer. They were to come confidently, boldly, with confidence that their requests would be heard and responded to. He invited both women and children to have a relationship with God equal to that of men. It was a revolutionary teaching which involved thinking not only at a higher level about God but also at a different level.

You can imagine the disciples' surprise when Jesus invited them to relate to *his* Father as *their* father. Relationships with authority figures were neither casual nor familiar. Jesus redefined the traditional relationship with God. Before, the relationship had been formal, distant, even frightening. Jesus taught the disciples to approach God the Father as he approached him, to enter into the inner circle of the Godhead. As the Father, the Son and the Spirit related to one another, the disciples were to relate to Jesus and his Father.

Later the apostle John would expand on the subject with his teaching regarding the believer as a "child of God." The disciples were to make themselves comfortable in the presence of God.

To approach God with such boldness would have been inconceivable to the disciples. To approach God with such simplicity would have been inconceivable as well. It would have been beyond the range of their expectations. What did Jesus really mean? What was he really saying?

To amplify his teaching in the prayer, later in the Sermon on the Mount, Jesus became more explicit. He specifically illustrated what he meant. Right across the page from the Lord's Prayer in most of our Bibles, Matthew recorded that Jesus taught the disciples to . . .

> *Ask* and it will be given to you; *seek* and you will find; *knock* and the door will be opened to you. For everyone who asks receives; he who seeks finds; and to him who knocks, the door will be opened. (Mt 7:78)

As to what Jesus meant, he left no doubt in the minds of his hearers. They were to have a radical new relationship with God the Father based on the same access Jesus had as his Son.

In chapter four we emphasized the nature and character of the Father. In the phrase "give us this day . . . ," the focus shifts to the nature of our relationship with him. The emphasis changes from the kind of person we expect a parent to be to the kind of relationship we expect between ourselves and our parents.

In terms of our inquiry, the key question becomes: How does the quality of our relationships with our parents affect the quality of our relationship with God, the Father, our heavenly parent?

A Relationship That Is "Askable"

Jesus said, "Ask and it will be given to you. . . ." Some children would never think of asking their mother or father for much of anything. They already know the answer. When parents always say yes, always say no or always says yes and no at the same time, it's possible for a child to experience their parent(s) in such a way as to preclude asking them for much.

☐   *Some parents say yes too easily.* They are so permissive that their responses limit their ability to parent effectively. If you were parented by a permissive mother and/or father, there are predict-able consequences for you as an adult.

If there ever was a permissive parent, an acquaintance of mine fits the bill. His teen-age son can do almost anything he pleases, and the father simply adapts accordingly. On one occasion the father even bailed his son out of jail after the son had let scores of traffic tickets go to warrant. When the son was stopped by the police for speeding, he'd been arrested because of the previous unpaid tickets.

According to the mother, when the son and the father talked on the telephone after the son's arrest, the entire emphasis of their conversation was on the son's proclaimed innocence that he hadn't been speeding when the police stopped him. They both sidestepped the whole issue of the unpaid tickets.

The son had lied time after time to the father about the tickets. When the son was arrested, the father paid the fine and bailed his son out because he couldn't stand to think of his son spend-ing the night in jail. There were no consequences for the son's behavior. The father shielded him from anything difficult or pain-ful.

Several months later, the son's auto-insurance rates quadrupled when he became an assigned risk. The father paid the added insurance costs without holding his son accountable. The father said yes to anything and everything the son asked. He was the permissive father, and theirs was the quintessential permissive relationship.

The son is the "pampered child" of chapter four.

It would be easy, would it not, for the son in this story to think that God exists to make life easy for him. God, like the father, is at the end of a chain waiting to be notified that the son has a need. All this young man has to do is pull, and God is expected to respond.

God doesn't always "come when we call him," at least not in the way this father responds to his son. God's answer to our prayers can be no, even when we think it should be yes.

Suppose we pray for the healing of a loved one dying of cancer, and the person dies. Anger under such conditions is understandable. If our idea of God is predicated upon a permissive parental relationship, the anger will turn to an abiding resentment toward God even years beyond the hurt or disappointment.

We pray for a job, and it doesn't come through. We ask for what we want, and it seems that God doesn't hear. As with the prayer for healing, after enough negative answers we become bitter.

The fault lies not with God but in the perception our relationship with a permissive parent fosters about our relationship with God. God is not an anxious mother in a nearby room waiting for our infantlike cry of discomfort. Like an infant, we too quickly and easily equate discomfort with need.

Whenever our relationship with our parents develops in such a way that we learn to presume upon their good graces, to take their kindnesses and their mercy for granted, it is likely that we will develop a similar relationship with God. Boldness becomes arrogance. Confidence becomes smugness. Prayer becomes exhibitionism, and our approach to God is distorted by their permissiveness. We question God's motives rather than our own. Our focus is on the one who is supposedly withholding what we deserve or, at least, expect. We're spoiled, and our relationship with God bears the consequences of our parents' permissiveness.

☐ *Some parents say no too easily.* In an earlier chapter, we identified these parents as authoritarian. Their children perceive them as punitive. These parents carry a big fist.

Later in our relationship with God, the "big fist" is projected onto God, and we relate to him as if he were the great bully in the sky. The effects of such parenting on our relationship with God are obvious. We decide to avoid him.

I'm more interested in a more subtle form of parental authoritarianism: when a parent's first response to any request by the child is no. No matter how legitimate the child's request, the response is the same: "The answer is no."

My memories of my grandfather fit just such a relationship. He was a stern, inexpressive man who demonstrated little warmth toward me other than anger. He was a good man but hard. He could be mean. Mostly, he said no.

Because of his obstinacy, in the early years of my relationship with him I learned not to ask anything of him because I could predict his answer. Instead, I asked my grandmother or my mother because they were more likely to say yes if they could.

In terms of our relationship with God, the natural consequence of growing up with such authority figures is not to bother God with our problems because we assume he'll ignore us, reject us or even abandon us. The person is waiting to be rebuffed by the God who is like the negative parent. Clearly, it's hard for that kind of person with that kind of parental relationship to love that kind of God.

☐ *Some parents say yes or no in the form of a double message.* Let me explain what I mean by *double message.* Years ago I had a client whose mother was a master of the double message. I remember one particular instance in which my client, a man in his late twenties, brought his girlfriend home for his parents to meet. The weekend seemed to go well until the last few hours before he and his girlfriend were to leave. His mother became increasingly critical of him and hostile toward his girlfriend. When they finally left the mother's home, the air was filled with angry words, accusations and rejections.

He arrived at his own apartment only to have his mother call him on the phone. Her voice was filled with rage. How could he bring "that kind of woman" home with him? He asked what she meant by "that kind of woman." The mother's response was vague and unclear. She just didn't like her.

The mother had begun the weekend saying yes to his relation-ship with the girl and had ended the weekend with a bitter no.

It was only a short time before he broke off his relationship with the young woman. It wasn't worth the pain it created for his mother.

His next visit home to see his parents surprised him. His moth-er spent at least part of an evening meal questioning him as to why he was in his late twenties and unmarried. Why couldn't he find "a nice young woman, marry, settle down and have babies"? She was ready to be a grandmother. His mother was critical of his being single.

He couldn't win! Her yes's and her no's were confusing. She was predictably unfathomable. The harm (which eventually brought him to therapy) came when he tried to make sense out of what really wasn't sensible. Over the years the double mes-sages, especially from his mother, accumulated inside him to the place where he ceased to function comfortably with others. He was confused, often alienated and distrustful.

When you talked with him, he would focus on himself, but not in a selfish sort of way. As the receiver of double messages, he felt it was his duty to please the message sender, and this made him self-conscious. It never occurred to him to question the validity of the message or the motive of the sender.

We would expect this young man's relationship with God to be confusing. He would love God, only later on to hate him. There would be a push/pull quality to it all. The young man would be plagued with a hot-and-cold kind of experience.

An example of what I mean occurred at a conference I attended. The main speaker, a noted pastor, was expositing from 1 Corinthians 13, the great "love chapter" of Scripture. However, as the pastor spoke, he took occasion to blast and criticize Pentecostals and charismatics for their position regarding the Holy Spirit. In so doing, he took God's words on love and used them hatefully. What the pastor was saying about love and how he was saying it were incompatible. A sincere listener in the audience would have been confused. How can loving words be used hatefully? If the listener trusted the pastor's words as "right teachings from God," the push/pull, love/hate double message would confound that believer's relationship with God. What goes around, comes around.

Secondly, we would expect him to be discouraged, even depressed. His thinking about God would be jumbled. He would work hard in his relationship with God only to stop trying at other times. He would not necessarily be resentful of God, nor fearful of him, but he would be confused and distrustful of God's motives toward him. Clearly, it would be hard for him to love God.

James hints at a relationship that is "askable" in the healthy sense when he writes, "Above all, my brothers, do not swear— not by heaven or by earth or by anything else. Let your 'Yes' be yes, and your 'No,' no, or you will be condemned" (Jas 5:12). Clearly, a healthy relationship is one in which the situation—not the bias of the person being asked—dictates the answer. In such a relationship, you can trust the answer to mean what it appears to mean on the surface. There isn't some hidden meaning to the reply which you have to intuit in order to understand it. A healthy relationship is open to reason; dialog and discussion are appropriate. When a decision is made, you can depend on it. Yes means "yes," and no means "no."

A Relationship Is Accessible

Jesus also taught that we are to *"seek the Father and we will find him."* What does he mean and what difference does it make in terms of our discussion? I take the meaning to have something to do with the accessibility of God.

Keep in mind the distance that existed between the God of the priests and the Levites and the ordinary Jew at the time Jesus was speaking. Keep in mind, also, the authoritarian nature of hierarchical relationships in his culture.

An accessible relationship is one in which you can find *who* it is that you are looking for. It has to do with the present versus the absent or neglectful parent. In this sense of the term, *accessibility* has something to do with a child's feeling secure. Whether or not it's accurate, the child's perception of the parent's presence is what matters.

Suppose, for example, a parent is busy doing the work of God. He is a pastor or a missionary. If children perceive that the parent can't be there for them when they need him, the child may appear to accept his absence on the surface but at another, deeper level, may resent the absence.

Those of us who counsel preachers' and missionaries' kids can tell all kinds of stories about the effects of this kind of parental neglect. The deadliness of the neglect lies in the motives of the parent. The child-become-adult can't just get mad at their parent without getting mad at God in the process. Why? Because the parent was really saying, "God made me do it." As adults the preachers' and missionaries' kids are often mad at God.

In addition to the matter of security, the matter of dependability arises as well. It takes the form of "people just can't be trusted to be there when you need them. You have to learn to take care of yourself."

If God is inaccessible, you learn to live your life independently of him.

A second emphasis in terms of our accessibility to God has to do with a relationship in which you can't find *what* it is that you need. Children rightfully expect their parents to be a source of nurture and comfort. Parents should represent a safe place, a relationship where you can go when you're hurt, a place of healing.

Unfortunately, many children experience a relationship that is qualitatively different. In place of nurture, they receive information and direction. In place of comfort, they experience judgment and hand slapping. These children learn very quickly to keep their mistakes and pain to themselves. They learn not to share, not to open themselves up to criticism, however well-meaningly it is given.

This is not to say that instruction and criticism are not important; the harm comes when a parent reverses the appropriate order. Comfort, in order to be effective, must come before instruction, and acceptance must come before criticism.

Suppose my daughter returns home after a date, crying and upset. She and her boyfriend have broken up, and she's shattered. Under those conditions it's easy to tell her what she needs to know about coping with men and to criticize her for her choice of boyfriends in the first place. After all "it's only puppy love, and he was a jerk all along." She can always do better.

If that's my immediate response, the likelihood is that the next time she comes home with bad news, she will not seek me out to tell me when she's in trouble. What she needs from me is to reach out to her in her pain, however trivial it may seem to me, and to accept her as she is at the moment. Instruction and direction can come later.

The reality, for many of us, is that instruction did precede comfort and criticism did precede acceptance. As a consequence, our relationship with God operates mostly at a cognitive level. Our relationship with God is based upon data rather than upon a sense of bonding. Facts have primacy over feelings, rather than operating in concert with one another.

The Scripture becomes a book of instructions before it is a book of comfort. We anticipate judgment to precede mercy.

Under these conditions a relationship with God becomes sterile, cold and impersonal rather than warm and personal. Some would even question whether or not it constitutes a relationship at all.

In addition to the issues of comfort and nurture are the issues of freedom and responsibility. Parents should work themselves out of a job; it's something their children need. In this sense a relationship is to rotate from a parent/child axis to an adult/adult axis. My daughter will always be my daughter, but in a healthy sense when she becomes an adult she ceases to be my child. I will always be her father but no longer her parent.

She needs to experience a growing sense of her own freedom from me, not only in the sense of independence but also in the sense of self-reliance. She needs to learn to shoulder her share of the responsibilities of an adult's world.

Some adults, however, still function as children in that they are unable to manage their freedom and they are unable to sustain themselves as self-reliant human persons. They are irresponsible and dependent.

Under such conditions, the irresponsible and dependent person's relationship with God appears on the surface to be a model of trust. However, trust and dependency are not the same. Genuine, informed trust comes only when we have the choice to decide otherwise. The dependent person doesn't have a choice. They believe that to remain childlike is the same as to "come as little children."

In terms of their relationship with God, everything will go well until too many things go wrong at the same time. Under these conditions, their inability to sustain themselves rises to the surface and their dependency takes its toll. God is blamed because he can't be trusted, and he can't be trusted because he hasn't rescued them from what they, themselves, are responsible for.

God's accessibility is not a substitute for our responsibility. Because we are to seek him does not preclude our responsibility to exercise self-discipline and sound judgment. To trust as a child would trust is not the same as remaining a dependent child. Those who do, find their relationship with God clouded with issues arising from their immaturity. They can love God if he takes care of them. They find it hard to love him when they are expected to take care of themselves.

A Relationship That Is "Approachable"
Jesus' third offer is his invitation for us to "knock and it shall be opened to you."

An approachable relationship is one involving a relationship with appropriate emotional boundaries. The concept of "boundaries," as it is used in the family-therapy literature, refers to the kind of indicators that mark off where one person ends and another person begins. Boundaries may involve physical space or time. Ultimately they represent an emotional issue.

For example, in the case of an infant, boundaries between the baby and the mother are blurred. In fact, the infant is unable to tell where he or she stops and the mother begins. From the infant's perspective, there are no boundaries between the two. That's O.K. It's appropriate. But when infants become young adults and their mothers treat them as if they are still children, then the blurred boundaries are inappropriate.

Years ago a friend reported to me the temptation to read her daughter's diary. The temptation was especially great because she was experiencing a great deal of her daughter's rebellion as hostility between herself and the girl. As the mother stood in her daughter's room, diary in hand in the middle of the day, she opened its pages and began to read. Almost immediately she realized that she was making a mistake.

Whatever she found out about her daughter's behavior she could never use because she was violating her daughter's space. Realizing her error, the mother replaced the book where she found it and went about cleaning the bedroom. She never found out what was written in its pages because to do so would have breached the emotional boundaries between her daughter and her. Had the daughter found out about the mother's reading her diary, the loss would have greatly outweighed the gain. The mother decided to respect the boundaries between her and her daughter.

On the one hand we are encouraged to make our presence known. We are not to be timid. God is not put off by our presence. On the other hand we are to respect the differences between ourselves and him. Our boldness is not to lead to rudeness.

The second issue implicit in the metaphor of "knocking" involves a relationship with appropriate hierarchy. The veteran family therapist Jay Haley talks about the need for children to learn that parents and children are qualitatively different from one another when it comes to issues of power.

Children should never succeed in dividing parents one from another, and they should never succeed in ruling over their parents. Healthy children learn to respect their parents' boundaries and to acknowledge their parents' authority.

Suppose a child bursts into the parents' bedroom when they were thinking of having sex. What are the adults to do? First of all they shouldn't make a federal case of it. Secondly, they should remind the child that when their door is closed, the child should respect their privacy and knock before entering. Last of all, they should consider putting a lock on their door. They should enforce their boundaries and their right to be treated with respect. The latter is what I mean when I refer to *appropriate hierarchy.*

Comfort or Discomfort?

Sometimes it's hard to love God because our relationship is one of fear and distrust. If we were the child who burst in on our parents and were yelled at and humiliated, we wouldn't understand why. We would have no idea what sex is all about. As a result, we would feel intrinsically uncomfortable and intrusive in any authority's presence. We'd believe, down deep inside, that God doesn't want us around and that we are unworthy.

If, in contrast, God the Father is askable, accessible and approachable, it will be easier to love him because our relationship with him is secure. He is patient and predictable.

It will be hard to love him if our relationship with him is otherwise.

CHAPTER NINE

WHEN WE FEEL LONELY

*U*s . . . *our* . . ."

Imagine you're at a party. The hosts for the evening bring out a table game they've recently discovered and ask everyone to play. The game requires that the guests divide into groups and really work together in order to win.

Halfway through the game, one man seems to disappear from the table. His wife gets up to look for him and finds him in the family room watching television. He didn't want to play anymore and hadn't thought to tell anyone what he was going to do. Returning to the table, his wife mutters, "He's just that way. We'll have to continue on without him."

"He's just that way."

This man lives his life as a single person even though he is married. He eats when he wants to eat and what he wants to eat. His family, following his lead, eats at random times during the day—rarely together.

Likewise, the man watches television when he wants to, and he watches what he wants to. When his children objected to his choice of programs, his solution was to buy them all television sets of their own. Nights come and go with everyone in their own rooms passively watching the programs they choose. They live as strangers.

The illustration would be sad even if it described one isolated family. The sadness is even more tragic because it describes a situation that is becoming the norm for the American family. Most of us are doing our own thing. We don't talk. We don't interact. We don't work together. When our families fall apart, we suffer alone.

If the husband in the story prayed the Lord's Prayer, what would it mean to him? I suspect this husband/father would pray the prayer with the same bias. Because he lives as a single, he would pray as a single.

You may remember I'm an only child of a single parent. My natural tendency is to be more like this man than unlike him. It wasn't until I began to think about the subject matter of this book that I realized that I prayed the Lord's Prayer using the plural pronouns *us* and *our* but what I really meant was *me* and *my*.

Imagine how the meaning of the prayer is changed when we pray, "give me this day my daily bread" rather than "give us this day our daily bread." Even though the meanings are so different, it's possible to say these pronouns without ever taking their significance into account.

How can this be?

The answer, again, lies in understanding our culture. We must ask ourselves the question, what affect does my living when I do, where I do, and how I do have upon my ability to love God?

Pervasive Culture

Like the air we breathe, our culture is always there and always persistent. Normally, we are oblivious to its presence. Only when our culture is somehow threatened do we seem to notice it at all.

The discomfort that comes when we find ourselves gasping for air is similar to what happens when our culture is crowded or overwhelmed by another. As long as we're in the culturally dominant position, we can breathe unconsciously. When we're in the culturally submissive position, we gasp for our cultural breath, even to the point of wondering if we'll survive. Actually, we're going through "culture shock." The natural response is to fight to preserve our culture and to restore our comfort.

Years ago my wife and I spent most of two summers in the Philippines doing short-term missionary work with several teams of college-age young people. It was the first time most of us had experienced a foreign culture. What an exciting yet confusing time!

What amazed me most was the amount of time it took me as supervisor to iron out simple adjustment issues that kept our young people from fitting into the Philippine culture. Even though our stay in the Philippines would only last two months, the collision of the two cultures was noticeable. Some of our young people became lethargic and barely productive. Others became quarrelsome and combative. Still others took the occasion to "fall in love" with one of their Philippine hosts or hostesses and began to talk about marriage. It was a challenging time.

Because of my bewilderment, I sought out a veteran missionary for advice. He explained how the established missionary community dealt with its own culture shock.

A significant portion of the time and effort of those missionaries who had lived in the Philippines for years was spent maintaining their American culture. Their children attended an American-type school. The families played American sports and games, celebrated American holidays, and ate, for the most part, American meals. The missionaries tried, much to their frustration, to keep American-type schedules. The end result was that many of the long-term missionaries lived with constant tension and frustration. He concluded, "If we as veterans have difficulty adjusting, what makes you think that your young people can adjust in two months?"

To further elaborate the point, he described two senior missionaries. One woman had dedicated her life to the evangelism of Philippine children. Her frustration came when she would use her American-tested, tried-and-true methods of child evangelism, only to find them meet with limited success in the Philippine context. She usually responded by upbraiding the Philippine Christians for not caring about children and by pushing herself harder to accomplish the work. More often than not she felt herself to be a failure as a missionary.

In terms of the culture, what she failed to see, and even refused to take into account, was that Philippine children never think of themselves apart from their family context. They never see themselves as individuals, only members of a broader, adult-dominated family.

Therefore, the child-evangelism methods of our American culture, with their emphasis upon a child's making a personal, individual commitment to Christ, didn't fit in the Philippine context. Philippine children tend to think and act as the adults in their families want them to think and act. If the significant adult makes a decision, then the child is free to do so as well. If the significant adult doesn't, then the child won't either. The missionary's frustration was inevitable.

Then he told me of a senior missionary who had lived in the Philippines for more than twenty years but had never learned the language of the indigenous people. Since most of the Philippine people he ministered to spoke and understood English, he felt it unnecessary to learn their language. Thus, Sunday after Sunday he preached and taught in English, only to see his congregation languish in number.

Much to his chagrin, a younger missionary with his mission group spent three years learning the Tagalog language. It was immediately obvious that nationals were more responsive to the younger missionary. Even though the young missionary often spoke in English and rarely preached in Tagalog, he implicitly understood their culture better and was able to relate more easily. The one missionary had grasped the importance of language acquisition in the understanding of culture, and the other had not. At the time of our short-term encounter with their mission agency, the tension between the younger and the older missionary had become an open sore and our participation in their projects a part of the conflict.

As for our own culture shock, it became obvious to me that our team was using American methods that had marginal validity in the Philippine context. Culturally bound because we didn't speak the language, we too could only expect frustration. My agenda as the supervisor changed from achieving great things for God to getting us through the experience in one piece. Fortunately, we survived the experience and grew as world Christians in our appreciation for the task of spreading the gospel.

I draw attention to these examples for a reason. Failing to take into account cultural differences between peoples can have disastrous consequences. The woman missionary disregarded differences in forms and methods; the senior missionary downplayed language and meaning. The failure to recognize the pervasiveness of culture dramatically influenced their communication of the gospel.

Unfortunately, culture shock is not limited to people who leave their own country. Many of us are in "culture shock" when it comes to our relationship with God. We attempt naively to "live," even accommodate, the foreign culture of the New Testament, only to find ourselves suffering from the disparity between then and now.

Common logic tells us that to take up residence in a culture as roughhewn and as alien as the one in the New Testament, serious adjustments would have to be made. All the same, some of us are guilty of the same ignorance in terms of forms, methods, language and meaning as the missionaries just mentioned. They became frustrated and disillusioned; so do we. One casualty might be our relationship with God.

Perhaps of any phrase in the Lord's Prayer, *our daily bread* most calls us to examine the cultural influences on our spirituality. In this chapter and the next, we will examine this phrase in terms of the cultural issues which I believe are implicit in the text of Scripture.

The Demands of Community

First of all, the prayer was meant to be prayed in the plural. The *we, us* and *our* of the prayer bring to mind words like *community* and *neighborhood.* In our day and age, we tend to think of a community as a place. A neighborhood has a radius and a diameter. We are thinking geographically. In contrast, in parts of the world which are less developed, less sophisticated and more rural than ours, *community* is a people and *neighborhood* is a relationship. The key dimensions are "who and what" rather than "where and when." Their world is different than our world because their view of the world is different.

The culture of Jesus' time was a culture where a man or a woman would live and die within less than a hundred miles of where they were born. Their life expectancy was less than half of ours. In such cultures, even today, the word *community* means something qualitatively different than in a culture involving social security, Medicare, frequent-flyer programs and discount vacations on Florida beaches. The Mount of Olives and Disneyland are more than centuries apart. They represent a difference in lifestyle as well as a difference in time and place.

☐ *In Jesus' day living in community meant needing each other.* When life frequently depends upon the consistency and productivity of your neighbor, the quality of your relationship becomes preeminent. There was no such thing as an individual. Whether it was farming, fishing or even buying and selling, the people of Jesus' time needed one another. Therefore, they cared for one another. That they would pray together, in concert with one another, reflected their community lifestyle. Belonging to a community wasn't a luxury; it was a necessity.

Our day and age has made a hero of the Marlboro man. The frontier individualism of the American West forms the fabric of our culture. Whether it's the investment bankers of Wall Street or the micro-chip entrepreneurs of Silicon Valley, the freedom of the individual is the name of the game. Our heroes walk alone.

The net effect for our spirituality is that whatever we might learn about God by being dependent upon one another is lost. Men and women implicitly believe that they must work out their problems on their own, often as a badge of their spirituality. Women's Bible study leaders and their male pastors denigrate those who through Bible study and prayer can't get the victory over depression, anxiety, relational conflict or whatever else ails them.

There is something about God we can't know apart from relationships with other people. People pull both the best and the worst out of us. We can't hide from anger or anxiety when they spring up as sarcasm toward our co-workers or smothering control of our children. Left alone, we can fantasize about God and delude ourselves about our relationship with him. Our relationships with real people illuminate our lack of trust and our fear of vulnerability. Community, or a life together with others, presses reality in upon us. Forgiveness, mercy and grace take on tangible, demonstrable meanings. The words grow larger than theological categories or biblical verses to be quoted like Tibetan chants. Our relationship with God at the macro level is mirrored at the micro level in our relationship with others. The demands of community expose the myths of a life alone.

☐ *When we live in community we are responsible for our relationships with one another.* The key thought here is the dimension of responsibility. It's one thing to be in a relationship with another person. It's another thing to take responsibility for the health and welfare of the relationship between you.

Recently, I counseled a young couple who had been married for about five years. The husband freely admitted that he was spoiled when he got married and that he was still spoiled. His single-parent mother had doted on him from the day his father had divorced her. The son had expected his wife to treat him accordingly. He had married a "mother" and, in his opinion, she was failing as a wife.

On the other hand, the wife was a no-nonsense kind of woman. *Duty* was her middle name. She oozed responsibility. Whatever he didn't want to do, she did. She worked hard and rarely laughed. There was very little play in her. In some ways they were a perfect match.

The presenting problem that sent them to me was his boredom. He had come to the conclusion that because they shared so little in common, there was no reason to stay married. When he announced this, she was caught completely off guard. She had arranged for counseling the next day.

In the process of our discussion, it became clear that he thought she should be responsible for him. For the most part, she agreed. He was living as a "married single," and she went along with his definition of the relationship.

The difficulties came because no one was responsible for their relationship—who they were and what they did when they came together. The husband was only in the marriage for himself, and the wife was only in it for him; taking care of someone isn't the same as having a relationship with the person. In terms of ultimate responsibility, no one "owned" the marriage. They hadn't even thought in those terms. Their task in counseling was to figure out what a marital relationship is and how to take care of it.

In our relationship with God, many of us are like the young man or young woman in this story. Either we expect God to take care of us (read "spoil" if it's appropriate) or we expect ourselves to take care of God as if he can't take care of himself. We live as "spiritual singles." The relationship between us is a mystery.

We may ask of him or we may work for him, even sacrifice for him. We are dependents or servants but never friends. What was missing for the young couple was the element of friendship. They could even simulate closeness sexually, but they couldn't experience it emotionally. Closeness is a relational dynamic best described as a function of friendship.

Where do we learn the reciprocity of relationship? Where do we learn to be responsible for others? Where do we learn to be responsible for the relationship between us? We do not learn it alone, but only in the content of community when we pray and mean "give . . . us . . . our. . . ."

To pray the prayer as a spiritual single is easy. To live the prayer in community is not so easy, but it is important to our knowledge of God and our relationship with him. Those who find it hard to love God are often those who try to go it alone.

☐ *Community should be inclusive rather than exclusive.* How big a circle shall we draw when we think of the inclusiveness of *we, us* and *our?* An exclusive circle will include only those persons with whom we are comfortable. They will speak our language, share our values and believe our beliefs. It's easy to live in community when its members are just like us.

However, the community that Jesus was forming when he taught his disciples to pray was to be much broader and diverse than what they had experienced and what they expected.

There is an interaction effect in the Lord's Prayer. The calculus of the *we, us* and *our* included the world of the Gentiles as well as the ethnically comfortable world of the Jews. The plurality of the pronouns anticipates the evangelism of and the conflicts between the Jews and the Gentiles recorded in the book of Acts.

The family of God would become diverse and boundless in terms of gender, race, status and nationality. God loved the world, and he expected his people to make the people of the world feel included and welcome. They were to feel at home.

In a small sense of the word, that's why it's more comfortable for us to pray the prayer in the singular. We only have to deal with ourselves. I don't have to deal with you, and you don't have to deal with me. Even more, we don't have to deal with "them," whomever "they" are, if they are different from us.

In contrast, the gospel breaks down the walls between us, or at least it's supposed to. If it hasn't, perhaps we should ask ourselves why not. Whatever the implications of the inclusiveness of the gospel, the least that is implied is that those who believe in God should live together in unity, and unity implies diversity.

The demands of community as expressed in the plurality of the pronouns reminds us that throughout the Scripture, God has always made a place for the stranger and the sojourner. There were to be no homeless. The poor were to be allowed to glean without shame. The rich—without being arrogant about it—were to make sure that there was enough left over for the less fortunate to find and keep. Even the alienated and the endangered were to have cities of refuge. People who loved God were safe people to be around. They were "given to hospitality," making room for others in their lives. They were to be inclusive.

On the other hand, when we live together as singles, the inclusiveness of the love of God shrinks to the size of the individual person. It's as if we can know all there is to know about the ocean if we hold a cup of salt water in our hands. If God's love can be held in the palm of our hands, it's not long before God, himself, is as small and insignificant as we shape him to be.

Living together, becoming responsible for our relationships and being an inclusive people is what community is all about. Living as a single, holding others responsible for our relationships and being ingrown and exclusive limits both life itself and loving God.

The degree to which our culture encourages individualism to the detriment of community is the degree to which our culture distorts loving God. The act of loving God most normally takes place within human experience where we rub shoulders with one another, sometimes as an expression of affection and other times out of irritation, but always as recipients of God's love, mercy and grace.

Loving God, therefore, is costly. You must give up your freedom to live alone if living alone means that others don't count because, functionally, they don't exist. Loving God means loving others and working at our relationships with them.

CHAPTER TEN

WHEN
OUR WORLD
IS CONFUSING

*D*aily bread."
Just as we find words like *Father* and *hallowed* simple before we really examine them, it is easy to assume the phrase *daily bread* means the same thing to everyone. Yet our cultural bias toward the phrase *daily bread* affects the way we live out the Lord's Prayer.

First of all, concepts of the word *daily* can be worlds apart. A student from Ecuador, South America, once explained to me that in the United States, with digital watches accurate to five seconds a month, people experience time differently than people do in his country, where the smallest measurement of time is the rising and setting of the sun.

On Sunday, church services in the bush are scheduled to start at eleven in the morning but could easily start an hour or two later. The people don't care because most have to walk to church, a long journey on dusty roads. If they arrive before the others come, they visit with whomever else is there.

Mealtimes, especially lunch and supper, can last for hours. After the meal there is always "siesta." He concluded that because people in his culture are less hurried, they are less harried as well. In Ecuador, people place the highest value on relationships; in American culture we give first place to productivity. Whatever the implications, it was clear from our conversation that time is a culturally subjective phenomenon—much more so than I with my technological and industrial bias had been willing to acknowledge.

The Dilemma of "Hurry Up"

The hardest adjustment my friend had to make in America was to the busyness of our society. Several times he teased me because of my preoccupation with starting on time, finishing on time and hurrying across the campus.

Had I been conscious then of what I know now, I would have stopped and listened to his words more carefully. He was trying to tell me something very important: You can't "hurry" life. All things come in their own good time.

Against the background of my friend's exhortations, we turn to the implications of the word *daily*. The culture of the Sermon on the Mount was more like the culture of Ecuador than ours. On the topic of time, American culture and New Testament Palestinian culture are radically different. The differences between the two are part of the dilemma we face when we seek to apply the meaning and patterns of Scripture to our lives.

First we must cope with the New Testament *emphasis on today rather than tomorrow*. When the disciples prayed for their daily bread, they were acknowledging their daily dependence on God. The fact that bread (before preservatives) had to be baked fresh every day unconsciously reminded them of their inability to ration their future. They were forced to think in terms of the here and now. What they didn't eat today would be gone tomorrow. It wouldn't last.

Our relationship with God is easily confounded because we have the ability to anticipate and control the practicalities of our future. When our freezers are full of food, our pantries are stocked to capacity, and our microwave ovens are at our beck and call, the urgency of the present is somehow blunted. When our anticipated retirement at age sixty-five is padded by social security and IRA's, something of the meaning of *daily* is lost.

This is not to say that we should reject the benefits of modern culture. However we must realize that the sense of urgency underlying our dependence on God is blurred when we are wrapped in a cocoon of modern technology.

I can think of one exception: parenting our children—especially when they become teen-agers. There seems to be a universal anxiety among Christian parents about their kids. The world seems much more dangerous today than when we parents were kids ourselves. The temptations are more deadly and the consequences more grim. Friends tell horror stories about the waywardness of their teen-age sons and daughters. The drugs, the alcohol and the unrestrained sex are temptations designed to shipwreck our children's lives.

Unfortunately for us, our children's security isn't something we can pull out of our freezers, pop in the microwave oven and serve when it's ready. Technology is useless in the areas of our greatest vulnerability. We can't control our kids' future. We find ourselves totally dependent on God. As parents, the greatest test of our faith is releasing our children to the process of growing up in a world we fear and even less understand. Under these conditions we come close to experiencing the meaning of the term *daily* as Jesus taught us to pray.

The younger generation, be they children, teens or young adults, face a similar anxiety. Their future is difficult to control as well. Nuclear weapons and a nuclear winter cast a pale over their tomorrows.

Knowing that tomorrow the world will not be the same as it is today provokes uncertainty. This uncertainty explains the younger generation's emphasis on present experience rather than on anticipating the future. They live for the "now" rather than for the future. Their "now" isn't the same as the sense of "daily" I'm suggesting. How it is different relates to the distinction between *the ordinary* and *the unusual.*

The ritual of the ordinary sacrifices of daily life and their significance describes the metronome-like quality of the word *daily.* I think of my father-in-law, who for years worked in the same place at the same job to support his family. Every Monday through Friday he got up in the morning, drove in his car, worked at his lathe and returned in his car to his home, only to repeat the sequence week after week for forty-two years. The same job at the same place with the same schedule. One thing is certain: His family, his wife and his children will forever understand the ordinary and dependable sense of the word *daily.*

I think it's interesting that my father-in-law has difficulty believing that the daily, dependable and ordinary doing of his work was, in fact, a ritual, a spiritual discipline honored and blessed by God. The baby-boom generation has an even harder time valuing the ordinary and dependable in the workplace. They expect their jobs to be stimulating and unusual. Few want to start at the bottom and work up. Even fewer are willing to do the boring work expected of entry-level workers.

It's not unusual for the baby-boomers to refuse to work in jobs without meaning for wages that are beneath their potential. Their heroes are the entrepreneurs who made their money fast and easy. Their generation has romanticized the world of work and career. Their dilemma is that there is very little romance in the ordinary course of human life, especially in the ordinary course of human work.

The popular answer to this problem for more and more people is to seek excitement outside of the world of work and routine, perhaps through the stimulation of chemicals or sexual excess. In this sense "now" is different from "daily."

Such people experience the emptiness of the extraordinary, because by definition, the extraordinary requires ever more of whatever is "extra" the next time around. For the unusual to maintain its excitement, an escalation effect must be built-in. It's only a matter of time before excess occurs and disillusionment appears.

The unusual, the extraordinary, the sensational, in whatever form it takes, is the drug of choice in today's world. The ordinary and dependable is shunned if it can be avoided and ridiculed when it surfaces.

In terms of loving God, there is something significant in our dependence on a wise Creator who has determined that the ordinary rituals of daily life are to have meaning to us because they have meaning and value to him.

Loving God is neither complex nor inaccessible. What makes it complex and seemingly beyond our reach is our tendency to approach God the way we approach life: looking for the extraordinary and the sensational.

In our culture, sometimes it's hard to love God because loving God seems mundane. It is unexciting when contrasted with the thrills of loving the gods that surround us: money, power, sex and status. These gods offer more excitement, bigger thrills and great-er variety. Loving God is hard in a context of sensationalism. If we're looking for excitement there are other gods to love.

The Dilemma of "Need"

The second difficulty we face because we live when and where we do centers on necessity or need. Jesus taught his disciples to ask their Father for "bread," the staple of life. Their need for bread focused their attention on what they lacked. When we pray, our request for bread, because we lack so little, reflects issues that are far different for us than for them. What is "bread" for us was not "bread" for them. Our limited needs and high expectations places us in a dilemma when it comes to *generosity rather than hoarding*. We would expect the well off to be generous and the poor to hoard, but often it happens the other way.

In the New Testament very few people were rich and most were poor. Functionally, there was no middle class. Only the rich could afford the excesses associated with wealth. The rich could afford to throw things away. The poor had to use whatever they had in order to stay alive.

Not until the late 1800s, with the coming of the industrial age and the rise of the middle class, was the accumulation of material goods an option for more than a few people. In a world where there is not enough to go around, the distribution of material goods, or generosity, is necessary for survival.

Recently, my wife and I spent some time in Uganda, in eastern Africa. We visited that country and its marvelous people five months after a civil war had placed the present government in control. During the years of the previous government, hundreds of thousands of civilians were massacred. The economy collapsed, leading to the chaos of runaway inflation. Literally, during the war and afterward, the people lived day to day and hand to mouth.

One day, while driving along one of their back roads, we noticed that unattended mounds of vegetables, fruits and other perishables were stacked alongside the road. Beside the display was a basket to receive monies in payment for whatever was purchased by the passersby. The whole arrangement was on the honor system.

I asked our Ugandan host what kept someone from stealing food without paying for it. He answered that their experiences in the war and the deprivation that followed had taught them that they had to be generous with whatever excess they accumulated. If others didn't have money to pay for whatever they needed, all they had to do was ask and the excess would be distributed. It was culturally wrong to accumulate material goods, especially food, if others were in need. Stealing, therefore, was very rare because it was unnecessary.

Of course not everyone operated on the principle of generosity, but the average, day-to-day experience of the people exhibited and valued generosity rather than the hoarding lifestyle we experienced at home.

I couldn't help making the contrast with our own home country. White-collar crime is rampant. Shoplifting occurs at epidemic levels. Unless something's bolted down, it's likely to be stolen. In our culture it's appropriate for those who control the excess to hoard whatever is in short supply rather than give it away. Leveraged buy-outs (LBO's) exacerbate the greed of the upper and upper-middle classes. "Trickle down" theories of economics are institutionalized, and the rich get richer while the poor get poorer.

The irony is that in a country and culture where we seem to have more than we need, enough is not enough. The idea is to get more than you need and to keep it for yourself.

A never-ending pursuit of "more is better" leads away from

God rather than toward him. Riches are not bad in and of themselves if they don't become ends in and of themselves. We are
taught in the New Testament that we are responsible for our
neighbor's well-being, especially if we have the ability to meet
our own needs.

Thus, the dynamic which fuels the materialism of our age isn't
the presence of things, nor the *amount* of the things we have.
Our materialism is fueled by acquisitiveness and accumulative-
ness, and is based on getting more and keeping it, with the
emphasis on the latter.

Rather than loving God, we love *things* when we spend a dis-
proportionate amount of our time and energy trying to keep what
we have rather than sharing or giving it away. We love things
more than God when at the practical level they "own" us rather
than we "own" them.

The second phenomenon which makes it hard to decide what
is a necessity is *complexity rather than simplicity.*

The bread referred to in the Lord's Prayer was an unleavened,
unsalted, hard-crusted loaf baked early in the morning of the day
it was to be eaten. It was simple fare.

When we think of bread, we ask, "What kind? White, whole
wheat or rye? Italian, French or Bavarian? Thin-sliced or regular?"
The options of breads available are staggering, and the multiplic-
ity of our choice is a metaphor of the dilemma we face.

Our two automobiles are parked in the front of our house. One
is a fairly new Japanese four-door sedan. The other is a 1966 Ford
Mustang. If we were to look at both engines, the contrast would
be dramatic. The new Toyota's engine is large and complex. The
wires and cables cross to and fro from high-tech component to
high-tech component. No amateur could make sense of it all.

In contrast, the 1966 Mustang has a standard, straight, six-cylin-
dered, relatively simple engine. It's possible for a nonprofession-

al to understand its workings and fix it.

The difference between the two cars shows how much our world and culture have changed in a little over twenty years. We have gone from what was relatively simple and manageable to what seems beyond us. We can no longer wrap our arms around the world issues that confront us. As in fixing the cars we own, we need specialists and experts to take care of what we can no longer take care of for ourselves. We have learned to live with complexity as a fact of life. Though we can do more with our gadgets, we feel more impotent in our helplessness to fix whatever breaks.

If the world has changed in twenty years, imagine how it has changed in two thousand. In the first century, "bread" reflected a lifestyle based on predictable, simple choices. Did you have enough to sustain your family and to meet their needs, or was it necessary for you to do more? An invisible but obvious line marked the boundary between having enough and having too much.

The rising and the setting of the sun, the coming and the going of the tides established the temporal boundaries of the disciples' world. Distances were measured by how far a person could walk in one day. Life was simpler.

The complexity of our lives provides innumerable distractions in terms of our relationship with God. The very presence of choices multiplies our anxiety. Because there is more to choose from, there is more to take into account. Thus, there is a greater opportunity to make mistakes. It's hard enough to relax, let alone love God.

Second, the complexity of our lives makes it easy to be distracted. Because we have more to attend to, we attend to more. Our bustling world is so noisy we defend our sanity by trying to tune it *all* out rather than trying to discriminate the important from the unimportant. Unfortunately, the sounds that are easiest to tune out are the voices of those who demand the least from us: our children, our friends, our God.

Third, the complexity of our world is associated with the stress we experience. It's easy to get addicted to complexity. The physiology of stress indicates that it's possible for a person to become addicted to whatever stimulates adrenalin within our bodies because adrenalin itself is addictive. It's a small step from having too much to do to needing to do too much.

So choices, distractions and noise, and the stress of modern life are associated with the complexity that surrounds us. Simplicity, on the other hand, involves the limitation of choice, the deliberate reduction of noise and the intentional reduction of stress.

It's easier to love God when identifying priorities is easy. We can know whether we love God or we don't. When life is simple, our idolatry has nothing to get lost behind. When life is simple, it's easier to hear the still, small voice of God because there is less noise and more time to be silent. We're less stressed and because stress mutes our ability to see, to hear and to feel God's presence in our lives. Of course, to choose to live more simply is not automatically to love God more. To live more simply provides the options needed to make the choice.

Our many options force us to determine and choose *essentials over peripherals*. Bread was a necessity of life. You couldn't live without it. What constituted a "need" was clearly demarcated from what constituted a "want."

In a culture saturated with excess, it's easy for wants to feel like needs. In a culture complicated by complexity it's easy to confuse what is central with what is marginal. Think about your own life: How much of your time and energy is spent taking care of matters that are of diminishing value or marginal importance?

A friend became particularly agitated at her ten-year-old son

126

because, while running through the house, he had brushed against the dining-room table and knocked some petals from the flower centerpiece. As she was upbraiding him for his clumsiness, she looked at the table and then at his face. Suddenly she realized that she had planned to throw the flowers away anyway, but her son was of infinite value. She apologized to her son, and he ran outside to play.

Later, as we talked, she questioned her priorities. She had fallen into the habit of correcting her son irrespective of the reason she was correcting him. Her solution was to pause for just a moment and ask herself whether or not the issue was important enough to draw attention to. She was evaluating the difference between essentials and peripherals and applying it to a very important relationship.

People—and our relationships with them—are of central importance. The same holds true for our relationship with God. Yet we get sucked into the vacuum of ignoring God while at the same time we seek to serve him. We choose to study about God rather than communicate with him and to preach the gospel without letting it first touch our lives.

Much of our attention is deflected toward the edges of our lives rather than the center. Jesus said, "What good is it for a man to gain the whole world, yet forfeit his soul?" (Mk 8:36). What remains after all else is winnowed away is what counts.

As we close this chapter, go back and reread the parts that seemed to provoke you. What did you disagree with? What particularly caused you to stop and think? Use the ideas in the chapter in the same way I used the conversation with my friend from Ecuador to stimulate my thinking. Make yourself an active evaluator of your participation in our culture. Fight against the tendency to be passive, to let it "just happen."

To love God we must evaluate the lifestyles our culture tempts us with and make the choices that allow us to live differently, if that's what we must do. The choice is ours.

Loving God has to do with centering our lives on Jesus Christ as Lord. The whole of life, the whole of our culture pushes us in the opposite direction. Under those conditions, no wonder it's hard sometimes to love God.

CHAPTER ELEVEN

WHEN WE
LIVE WITH
UNFORGIVENESS

A *nd forgive us our debts, as we forgive our debtors."*

In the summer of 1971, my wife and I bought our first home. We had been married more than ten years and thought we would live in church-owned houses for the rest of our lives. A change of jobs allowed us to take that first big step. We borrowed the money for a down payment and signed the mortgage.

Our new house was located in northeast Orange County, approximately fifty miles from downtown Los Angeles. The neighborhood was stable, white, middle class and straight-arrow politically conservative.

I quickly busied myself with my new job as the executive director of an independent Christian mental-health agency. Lucy went about making the house a home, and our daughters, eight and three at the time, were excited about making new friends. It seemed like a dream come true for all of us.

Within two weeks we had a rude awakening—an incident between our eldest daughter and several neighborhood boys her own age.

Across the street from our house was a field of high grass about half the size of a football field. In years gone by, children had built a shed there. Our daughter Sheryl and one of her new friends loved to play in that dilapidated old shed, pretending it was their very own house.

However, unknown to Sheryl, the boys on the street thought the shed belonged to them. They were frustrated and angry with the presumptuous newcomers on their turf.

One day, when the young girls were playing house, the boys began to throw rocks and clumps of grass at the shed. The rocks thumped noisily on the roof and the clumps of grass rained dirt and dust down through the cracks.

To the delight of their tormentors, the two terrified girls ran for home, crying and shrieking. Sheryl burst through the front door of our house, screaming out her tale in between deep and dramatic breaths.

As Lucy tried to calm the two girls, my response surprised us all. I regressed to the methods of my boyhood youth.

"Listen, Sheryl. This is what you're going to have to do. I want you to go back to the shed. I want you to go inside, but before you do, I want you and your friend each to pick up a fist-sized rock in each hand."

My pulse rate quickened and the adrenaline began to flood my body as I laid my battle plans. I was back on the streets. The girls and Lucy were dumbfounded by my passion.

"Watch through the cracks between the boards. When the boys

come back (don't worry; they will), wait until they throw their rocks. Then, and only when you're sure they're done, burst out of the door, rocks in hand, and pick out the slowest, fattest boy of the lot, and run him down. Chase him until he falls down.

"When he falls, stand right on top of him, and with all your might both of you throw your rocks at him as hard as you can. Hurt him. Then they'll leave you alone. They'll be afraid to mess with you after that."

My whole body was trembling with emotion. I had devised the perfect counter move. The girls would defeat and humiliate their enemies.

Calmly, my wife looked me in the eye and then at the two terrified girls. She said, "Maybe before we start World War 3, we should try to find out why the boys are angry. Dennis, you settle down while I take the girls down to where the boys live and talk with them. Then, if all else fails, we'll bring out the heavy artillery."

She was right. Her calmer voice prevailed.

As it turned out, the children were able to make peace when one of the boys confronted Sheryl with his side of the story. She had been riding her bike and had inadvertently pushed him off the sidewalk and into some bushes. He got mad and decided to settle it the way boys often do.

Lucy negotiated a round of apologies, and the children settled into ten years of being best friends. The crisis passed.

What amazed me was how I so easily regressed back to my youth. Twenty years had gone by, fifteen of which came after I had become a Christian. I had graduated from a Christian college and seminary, where I had studied the Bible, theology and church history. I had served on the pastoral staff of a church for five years and was an ordained minister of the gospel.

All of this had been abandoned in the heat of the fight. My

131

adolescent operative principles of "Never forgive! Never forget! Never give up!" overwhelmed my reason at the moment. You may recall from an earlier chapter my grandmother's advice to defend myself when a bully beat me up. I was going far beyond my grandmother's advice; I was telling two little girls to stage the second battle in a neighborhood war.

Fortunately, my more thoroughly Christian wife saved the day and kept north Orange County from becoming a combat zone.

My memories of that regressive incident remind me that the phrase in the Lord's Prayer having to do with debtors and forgivers was included for folk like me. Admitting I'm wrong and doing something about it is easily said but often hard to do.

Debtors

In his model prayer, Jesus instructs the disciples to accept their relational obligations and failures. Indebtedness in this sense is similar to the issue of repentance. Repentance is the other side of forgiveness.

I'd like you to examine several types of debtors and how their strategies affect their relationships with God. Then, at the end of the chapter, be ready to ask yourself, "When it comes to handling my own indebtedness, which kind of strategy do I use and how does it affect my relationship with God?"

☐ *Debtors who try to avoid their indebtedness.* The most common way to deal with being indebted to others is to avoid the debt all together. Repentance never happens because the need for repentance is never owned. The issue is deflected somewhere else. The avoidance can take several forms.

One form involves *the deliberate debtor.* This person deflects needing to repent by saying, "It's your problem. You deal with it."

One of my clients refused to take responsibility for the hurt his wife was experiencing; he claimed she was too sensitive. When I probed deeper, it became clear that he habitually deflected most of the responsibility for their marriage problems onto her, and she was in the habit of accepting it. They had to work hard to get him to accept responsibility for more of their problems and get her to accept responsibility for less.

After many tears and much anger the couple worked their problems through, but only after the wife kicked the husband out of the house because he refused to acknowledge several extramarital affairs that had surfaced and because she came to believe that she had the strength to go it alone if need be. In terms of our discussion, he was a deliberate debtor.

A second pattern involves *the casual debtor.* These debtors discount the degree or severity of hurt they have caused others. They say, "No big deal. What are you so upset about?" Unfortunately, I fall into this category.

When Lucy and I first married, I habitually forgot to celebrate occasions such as Valentine's Day and Mother's Day. In my mind I was far ahead because I remembered Lucy's birthday, our anniversary and Christmas and only forgot the "unimportant occasions." When Lucy would get her feelings hurt, because those days were important to her, my initial response was, "No big deal."

What was at stake was the reality of her feelings of disappointment. Her feelings were real, even though I didn't think they were valid. My tendency to discount their significance was more hurtful than forgetting to celebrate the events. I was a "casual debtor," and my wife paid the price.

A third pattern involves *the unconscious debtor.* These people are unaware of their indebtedness.

One of my students confronted her father with her feelings of neglect. She had decided to tell him how she really felt because

133

she had been unable to erase her negative feelings. They were causing her progressively to withdraw from him.

She asked him to her apartment for dinner. When the opportunity came to place the matter out on top of the table, she was terribly nervous. Unable to sit down, she paced back and forth. Finally, her father asked if something was wrong. She sat down, took a deep breath and told him of her feelings and of the incidents she could remember that she had interpreted as his not caring. As her story unfolded she could see the tears well up in his eyes.

At the end of her discourse he simply said, "I'm sorry. I didn't know." He had been so preoccupied with his own career and agenda that he had neglected those around him. He was an unconscious debtor.

In terms of our overall indebtedness, our unconscious debts often are the greatest of all. To accept the likelihood of such debts and to recognize our need to repent of them, demands that we recognize our fallen humanity. We must also acknowledge the hurts we cause others even when we don't intend to. In this sense of the word, intentionality makes a difference only in a court of law. In the court of human experience we accrue debt in accordance with our behavior and not in accordance with our intentions.

☐ *Debtors who try to manipulate their creditors.* The next strategy, a form of avoidance, is important enough to warrant its own category. Some debtors rely on manipulation to resolve their debts. Manipulative people confuse sorrow with repentance. When they are wrong, they are genuinely sorry. Their key issue becomes whether or not they intend to change and will match their intention with behavior.

For example, in the area of domestic violence, sorrow is one step of a predictable cycle. First comes the accusation or verbal abuse of the victim. Then comes the violence or physical abuse, followed soon after by the abuser's embarrassment and sorrow, only to be followed again by the same pattern.

The abuser appears to be genuinely downcast and repentant during the sorrowful phase. The presence of sorrow is a poor indication of the abuser's commitment to change. Getting abusers to take steps to change involves getting them to behave differently in addition to feeling differently.

Breaking the cycle of abuse often involves helping the victim to recognize the difference between sorrow and repentance and to hold the abuser accountable for more than the first.

At a less extreme level, manipulation is our strategy whenever we say, "How can you be mad at me when I'm sorry for what I have/haven't done?" We think feeling bad is sufficient payment for whatever pain we've caused. Our sorrow removes the right of the aggrieved person to do anything other than forgive us. The issue shifts from one of justice to one of feelings.

Manipulative debtors are masters at redirecting the issue from their debts to their feelings. Often the people they've offended (those to whom the debts are owed) feel guilty because they are "causing" the debtors to feel bad and the debtors have suffered enough.

Manipulation is the most deadly form of avoidance of all. In my opinion, it is the fastest-growing form of avoiding responsibility in use today. It's the strategy of choice for the last two decades of the twentieth century.

□ *Debtors who blame others for their debt.* The next strategy for handling our indebtedness involves the very human tendency to blame others for our faults and mistakes. On the one hand, the person who blames others for his or her indebtedness accepts the "fact" of the debt but not the responsibility for it. The person says, "I'm wrong. But you, or someone else, or something else made me do it." The key lies in the disjunctive *but.* When the word *but* follows "I'm wrong," the person is rejecting ultimate responsibility.

Blame makes others responsible for our actions. The fulcrum of responsibility shifts from ourselves to someone or something outside ourselves. Even if we say "the devil made me do it," we have masked our dependency and have shifted responsibility to the shoulders of someone else. Our repentance is incomplete.

☐ *Debtors who are defensive about their indebtedness.* The defensive debtors may admit that they are wrong, but they do so with clinched fists. They are saying, "I may be wrong but so are you." Defensiveness doesn't shift responsibility for the debt to another, as is the case for blaming, but it does spread it around. Whatever repentance there is can only be partial because the responsibility is shifted just enough off-center to focus the attention on someone else too.

The "clinched fist" strategy removes the possibility of the accuser feeling justified or smug. Defensiveness achieves the goal of denying any sense of satisfaction on the part of the one to whom the debt is owed. If people with clinched fists ever apologized to you, you know what I'm talking about. There is a deflated quality to their apologies. Though they are saying they are wrong, their demeanor speaks otherwise.

☐ *Debtors who repent of their debts.* The last strategy for handling our indebtedness is repentance. It is the only strategy consistent with Jesus' intent for the prayer. To be forgiven of our debts we must accept the legitimacy of those debts. The person who repents says, "I'm wrong, and I accept responsibility for my actions and decisions." The acceptance of responsibility is matched with whatever behavior is indicated by the repentance. For example, in the case of alcoholics, repentance would involve their checking themselves into a hospital for treatment or attending an Alcoholics Anonymous meeting and beginning a twelve-step recovery program. Their intention must be matched with behavior.

Repentance is the stance of the tax collector described in the Gospels who stood in the Temple, beating his breast, saying "God, have mercy on me, a sinner" (Lk 18:13). Jesus says that his behavior was the behavior of humility. Both the attitude and the actions of repentance provoke God's response of forgiveness.

Forgivers

In the twenty-five years I've been a therapist, no other word has been bandied about in the Christian community more than the word *forgiveness*. Why? Because it's so central to a person's mental health. However, no other word has been so misunderstood and trivialized in its meaning. For me, forgiveness is a two-sided coin. The one side involves releasing people who have harmed you from your retribution for whatever they have done to you. The second involves releasing yourself from the need for retribution. The process involves both actions and feelings. Forgiveness, in this sense, is by no means easy—at least not as easy as it is held out to be by contemporary preachers.

Let me suggest several categories of forgivers in the same way we discussed the matter of debtors. Again, as you read, ask yourself which category best describes you. At the end of the chapter we'll discuss the relationship between loving God and the issue of forgiveness.

I'd like begin to discuss forgiveness at a rather unusual place: with the category of *those who shouldn't forgive*. Most Christians assume that forgiveness is an absolute. There are no exceptions. I beg to differ with these conclusions for at least two reasons.

The first reason has to do with the tendency for those who have been injured to forgive so quickly that they don't give themselves time to assess how profoundly they have been injured.

Consider a person injured in a serious automobile accident who is badgered into signing off on a settlement before he knows how badly he has been hurt. Later he finds that his injury is far worse than was assumed. Now it's too late to seek an adjustment because he has signed away his legal right to press for additional damages. He was too quick to forgive and the impulsiveness of his decision cost him dearly later.

The second reason involves the victim's feelings. Take, for example, a woman who as a young child was incested by her father. Her awareness of the incest surfaces when she discovers that her older sister had been incested as well. The conspiracy of silence that enveloped the family when she was a child envelops the family still. No one is willing to talk about it. The secret is to be kept hidden.

Only those who have suffered this kind of abuse know how profoundly they have been injured. The memories of the incest lie just beneath their emotional surfaces. In the case of the victim, her relationship with her father is affected, obviously. So is her relationship with her mother, whose passivity at the time exacerbated the situation. Most of all, her relationship with her husband and her feelings about herself are affected day after day in the here and now.

At some point she must make a choice about what to do with her memories and the feelings attached to them. Her Christian teachings prompt her to forgive her father.

She's been taught, "After all, didn't it all happen years ago? Aren't some things better left alone? What good will it do? He's an old man. Even though he still denies responsibility for whatever happened, why open old wounds? Just forgive him and be over with it."

This approach denies the validity of her feelings as the legitimate victim of a terrible abuse. The abuser refuses to repent and the family system colludes with the abuser to pressure the victim into precipitously forgiving him. The greater damage occurs when the woman's present situation is overlooked in the haste to relieve the consequences of the abuse of the past. The victim is victimized again.

I believe we have every right to hate whatever God hates. Child abuse is at the top of his list. It was Jesus himself who said, "But if anyone causes one of these little ones who believe in me to sin, it would be better for him to have a large millstone hung around his neck and to be drowned in the depths of the sea" (Mt 18:6). Strong words. Strong feelings. To forgive the abuser when he refuses to repent is to discount the severity of the abuse and to invalidate the feelings of the victim. Frequently, she is left with the residue of her unresolved anger and hurt while the abuser is freed of the consequences of his actions.

Instead of forgiveness, I coach the victim to "release" her anger and hatred to God—but only after she has accepted its validity.

Paul's teaching in Romans is paradoxically comforting in these cases.

Do not take revenge, my friends, but leave room for the God's wrath, for it is written: "It is mine to avenge; I will repay," says the Lord. On the contrary:

"If your enemy is hungry, feed him;

if he is thirsty, give him something to drink.

In doing this, you will heap burning coals on his head."

Do not be overcome by evil, but overcome evil with good. (Rom 12:19-21)

The paradoxical nature of Paul's teaching is that God's commitment to justice and his ability to extract vengeance releases the victim from extracting her own retribution. She need not forgive her abuser for whatever he has not repented of. It is the clear teaching of Scripture that repentance is a precondition to forgiveness (see Lk 24:47; 2 Cor 7:9-10). Instead, she must weigh the costs of holding onto her feelings, usually hurt and anger, and must ask herself if the effects of holding onto the feelings are worth the costs. To release one's anger and bitterness is different from forgiving the offender.

By leaving the debtor to God's judgment, the abuse victim can once again choose how she will relate to her father. For example, I find that traffic policemen usually are polite. Though they write big tickets as part of their duty to the legal system, they don't often throw in nasty comments of their own. And when I happen to see "Perry Mason" reruns on television, the bailiff who leads the prisoner into the courtroom treats the defendant with courtesy and respect. Policemen and bailiffs can respect both the accused person and the need for justice because these officers have confidence in the legal system; it is not their job to judge and punish. On the contrary, police harassment could get the case thrown out of court.

Many times we think that if we show kindness to someone who has wronged us, they're getting off free. We need to remember that they will stand before a Judge someday who will remember all the facts of the case. It is his job to judge and to avenge, and he will not shirk it.

The next category of forgiveness is similar to the first. It is *those who deny that they have been injured and therefore can't forgive.*

An illustration that comes to mind involves the death of a young child after a long, terminal illness and the church's response to the child's parents.

The pastor of the church had taught his parishioners that they were to thank God for everything and that the Lord was in control of all things, truths that on the surface seem right and appropriate. How these teachings were applied to the death of the young child is what is at issue.

The pastor told the young parents to rejoice in the death of their son, to sing hymns and give thanks. Any grieving on their part was interpreted as a lack of faith, even a sin against God.

As a result they could not grieve the loss of their child. Consequently, the young mother experienced a major depression and the marriage was severely stressed. Years later, the parents ultimately divorced.

Looking back, both partners recognized that the marriage had taken a serious turn for the worse when their child had died. Their need for comfort and their need to work through their hurt and anger had been short-circuited by their Christian teaching. They didn't forgive because they couldn't forgive. The reason they couldn't forgive was their belief that they had nothing *to* forgive. The triumphalism of their Christian teaching had kept them from dealing congruently with the reality of their life situation. The price they paid added to the loss of their child: It cost them their marriage.

There are more people in this category than we would like to admit, people whose need to forgive has been glossed over by the denial of their injury. My observation is that something snaps when the denial ceases to function and the teaching fails to work. The disillusionment of the ones who had embraced the teaching results in their spiritual burnout or their rejection of their faith. The focus shifts from the original injury to their need to forgive those whom they believe have deceived them. The focus becomes the church and its teaching.

The third category of forgiver is the counterpart of the defensive forgiver: *those who partially forgive but never forget.* I'm talking about grudging forgivers. They forgive but with clenched fists.

I know of couples whose marriages bear the weight of past sins which were supposedly forgiven but are obviously not forgotten.

I'm aware of sons and daughters who carry hatred toward their parents around in their viscera only to shrug their shoulders when asked if they have put the past behind them.

In particular, I'm aware of a father who supposedly forgave his son's poor business judgment which resulted in the loss of a great deal of the father's money. Now, whenever the simplest business decision arises, the father puts the son's past mistakes on the table and punishes him again for his failure. The son's response is to ignore his father and to avoid him unless it's necessary. To this day if you were to ask the father whether or not he had forgiven his son, he would say he had. If you were to ask the son if he felt forgiven, he would say he didn't. Partial or grudging forgiveness is worse than no forgiveness at all, at least from the perspective of the one who supposedly was forgiven.

This is not to confuse partial forgiveness with the limits of forgiveness. For example, a father who has abused his children shouldn't be left alone with his children if that has been the judgement of a court of law. A convicted felon shouldn't be given a license for a gun. Forgiveness, in this sense, has its limits, and these limits are forged, in the main, by common sense.

The fourth category, like the first, is not technically a category of forgiveness. However, it needs to be addressed because of its prevalence. It involves those who hate and, therefore, won't forgive. Hatred, and its companion bitterness, are expensive addictions. Not only is hatred an addiction, it's also an acquired taste, just like learning to eat onions or drink coffee.

I have really hated only one person in my life. I mean hatred that is obsessive. Hatred you can't let go of. The experience of hatred is still vivid in my memory. What I remember most of all is the addictive nature of the hatred. I got to where I liked thinking about my feelings toward the person. I fantasized about what I wished would happen to him. The thoughts about the situation that provoked my hatred wouldn't go away. I soon came to realize that the hatred was controlling me rather than me controlling it. I was hooked.

One night, as I was talking with my wife, I was able to get in touch with what really hurt me about the situation. The tears came, and she held me like a baby as I cried. When the emotion ebbed I knew I had to make a decision about my hatred. If I held on to it now I was choosing my own fate. I would be giving in to my addiction.

By God's grace I released my hatred in the same way I described above. I didn't "forgive" the person because he hadn't asked nor sought my forgiveness. Rather I took comfort that the God of heaven who valued justice would look after my interests. I needed to get on with my life. The hatred soon passed. I'd had a taste of hatred and its bitterness and, disconcertingly, had grown addicted to it.

So, whatever hatred is, I know what it can do to you and how it can grab you by the throat and control your life. I also know what's at stake if you don't find a way to let it go. The irony is that there comes a time when you become your own persecutor. Holding onto the hatred becomes an issue separate from whatever provoked the hatred to begin with. Unlike the kindly bailiff, you become your own jailer, perpetuating your own sentence as if it were open-ended, with no end in sight.

The last category of forgiveness is the most congruent of all. It involves *those who, though wounded, still forgive.*

I am amazed by the human spirit when it is bathed and energized by the grace of God. It's one thing for the Savior on the cross to forgive his persecutors. He had been prepared from all eternity for the task. I don't mean to diminish his act. I'm only saying that human persons by the grace of God are capable of incredible acts of forgiveness, as was Jesus.

Whether it's the forgiveness of a spouse for the waywardness of his partner or the forgiveness of a parent who has hurt you, forgiveness is possible. Forgiveness is the ointment God uses to heal broken relationships. It is the bandage used to bind wounded souls. Forgiveness is among the greatest gifts we can give one another.

Forgiveness for the small things in life is important too. It involves knowing when to be assertive about the quality of service and work you expect, and knowing when the people serving you are doing the best job they can. It involves knowing when to make a big deal about something and when to let the issue slide because people are more important than the principle involved.

Forgiveness is the Christ in us accepting others for what they are, rather than for what they ought to be. Forgiveness is making the love of God tangible in ways that can be experienced day to day and hour by hour. It is the way of Christ and the Christian.

Loving God and Our Locus of Control

How in the world can we repent and forgive this way? On the surface it appears to be possible but not probable. Most of us have trouble one way or another.

Dysfunctional debtors and forgivers share one significant characteristic in common: their emotional dependency. What I mean by *dependency* has to do with the matter of a person's "locus of control."

In emotionally mature people, the locus (or location) of control is perceived as being located inside themselves. They perceive themselves as neither victims nor persecutors. They take responsibility for their own actions and refuse to take responsibility for the actions of others.

On the other hand, such emotional habits as blaming and

defensiveness are indications that people perceive the responsibility for their actions, even their own beings, as lying outside themselves. Apparently whole and functional people tend to mask their emotional dependency with these two subtle mechanisms.

In therapy, I can tell people are really ready to grow when they are able to say out loud to themselves, to God and even to others that they take responsibility for their own actions and that no one else is responsible for what they do or how they feel. They "own" their locus of control. When people repent or grant forgiveness they are acknowledging that their locus of control lies inside themselves rather than outside. When responsibility is matched with behavior they show that they have resolved the matter of the locus of control.

I have come to believe that loving God and taking responsibility for our debts and our forgiving others are inextricably linked to one another. The locus of control is one step in the journey of loving God.

What Now?

Perhaps while reading this chapter you saw some negative patterns in your own life. Assuming you did, let me make several suggestions as to what to do next.

☐ *Identify your probable debtor strategy.*

Do you avoid taking responsibility for your actions? Can you remember arguments with people who seemed to be trying to convince you that you were wrong and you ignored them or tried to manipulate them? Is it just plain hard to say the words "I'm wrong"? Is it even harder to do something about it when you are wrong?

Maybe you get caught in the trap of blaming and defensiveness. If so, your conflicts with others will tend to be cyclical. That is, you seem to be arguing about the same things all the time. Only, sometimes it's your fault, and sometimes it's the other person's fault. Either way, it's tough to say "I'm sorry."

Our negative debtor styles, whether avoidance, manipulation, blaming or defensiveness, all lead to partial repentance at best and to lack of repentance at worst.

☐ *Identify your probable forgiveness category.*

The way in which we respond to the demands of forgiveness affects our relationships with others and with God as well. Go back and reread each section on forgiveness. Which one fits you best? What would the people who know you the best say about you? If you don't know, ask someone.

Look inside yourself. Is there someone toward whom you carry a grudge? What have you swept under the rug? Whom do you try to avoid and why? Pay special attention to the people who ought to be close to you and aren't. Why don't you keep in touch?

☐ *Do something about it.*

Repentance and *forgiveness* are words that have concrete behaviors attached to them. As you read the sections that went before, maybe a thought about someone or an idea of something you need to do came to mind. Why wait any longer? Why not do something about it now?

A television ad for running shoes comes to mind. After talking about the advantages of their product, and the advantages of physical exercise, the following words appear on the screen: *Just do it.*

How we choose to handle the issues of repentance and forgiveness determines a great deal about how we experience the reality of God's love. If we partially repent or partially forgive, for whatever reason, we complicate the process of loving God and hinder the process of loving others and being loved by them.

However hard it is, the locus of control for it all lies within ourselves. What is of greater importance is that you deal with the issues. Loving God begins with an appropriate taking of responsibility for what you need to own and an appropriate disowning of what you can't take responsibility for. Learning the difference between the two is what this chapter is all about.

CHAPTER TWELVE

WHEN WE STRUGGLE WITH SIN

A *nd lead us not into temptation, but deliver us from evil . . ."*

Most of Jesus' model prayer seems appropriate for any son or daughter to pray to a loving father—whoever that father might be. Jesus taught that the Father in heaven "gives good gifts to those who ask him" (Mt 7:11). You would expect that from a parent. Giving is a given!

Yet one aspect of the prayer is complex even on the surface. Why would you need to ask a loving father not to tempt you to do wrong? Why would you have to ask him not to test you? Whatever the answer is, it's not obvious.

For those of us who sometimes find it hard to love God, the enigma lies at the foundation of our suspicions. Down deep inside ourselves we believe that we really can't trust God. It's a hard saying, but it's true. Why might this be so?

My answer lies in the cynicism many of us feel toward God.

When an earthquake struck Soviet Armenia, more than a hundred thousand Armenians were killed and a million or more people were left homeless. Newscasts have been filled with reports of the human loss. Newspapers carry pictures of orphaned children wandering the streets searching for their mothers. It's a disaster of monstrous proportions.

This isn't the first tragedy to strike Armenia. In the early 1900s millions of Armenians were killed by the Turkish Army in a genocide that rivalled the atrocities of the Nazis toward the Jews during World War 2.

Hatred for the Turks still burns in the hearts of many Armenian zealots. Turkish embassies are bombed and their diplomats are assassinated because many Armenians still feel the pain of their holocaust. After the earthquake, one newscast showed a mother who had lost her children in the disaster cry out, "Why has God punished us again, after we've suffered so much already?"

The mother's cry, "Why God? Why me? Why us?" is neither new nor unique. Anyone who has suffered tragedy in one form or another knows the dread that fills your soul as you face the future. Before, you always assumed that God's hand would protect you and those you love from danger. His overarching lovingkindness would serve as a protective shield. Then comes the disaster. God's shield has failed. The worst has happened.

Not only must you deal with the emotions of the moment, the feelings of loss and grief, you must also deal with your feelings of abandonment. Where was God when you needed him? Why didn't he keep whatever happened from happening?

If you're a Christian, your doctrine of the sovereignty of God takes a beating. Isn't God in control of all things? What happened this time? Did he slip up? If God is a loving Father, why would you need to ask him not to lead you into temptation?

The cynic bruised by tragedy will answer, "Because you really can't trust anyone, not even God." For people whose doubt is not that full-blown, the issue festers like a sore in their spiritual beings. Though apparently small, this infection is painful and dangerous. You hope it won't spread and attack your faith, but you know that something's wrong because you can't recover the trust in God you once experienced.

No easy answer to the problem exists because it exposes the whole dilemma of the relationship between God and evil. Why does God allow evil to exist and even sometimes prosper? Why do the righteous suffer? Perhaps the answer lies somewhere in the reason for this strange request in the Lord's Prayer.

At least a partial answer surfaces if we understand the nature and purpose of testing, the nature and extent of evil, and, last of all, the nature and power of the enemy we face, Satan. These issues confound the process of loving God and multiply the hardness of the task. In terms of our discussion, it is food for thought.

Never More Than We Can Handle
When our difficulty in loving God comes from lack of trust, a solution to the problem may lie in understanding the meaning of temptation and the purpose of testing. What is the nature of the problem itself?

One thing we can be sure of, God will never tempt us to do evil. Scripture teaches:

When tempted, no one should say, "God is tempting me." For God cannot be tempted by evil, nor does he tempt anyone; but each one is tempted when, by his own evil desire, he is dragged away and enticed. (Jas 1:13-14)

To tempt anyone with evil would be inconsistent with the nature

151

and character of God. He is neither evil nor the source of evil. In terms of our discussion in the previous chapter, God is saying, "Don't blame me for your problems. Look to yourself first." It's a matter of the locus of control. We are responsible for ourselves and for our own actions. Yet the implication of the prayer is that we need to petition the Father for something. But what?

Most commentators agree that the petition has to do with testing rather than temptation. The petition of the prayer is the request not to be placed in a position of being tested beyond our limits. It involves asking God not to put us in a place that is beyond our ability to handle. God does not tempt but he does test.

This distinction may or may not be comforting, depending upon our level of cynicism. If the infection is deep and pervasive, it makes little difference whether or not God tempts or God tests. Either way God is the active agent and we are the recipients. If the infection is just beginning to spread, our perceptions of God's intention is open to interpretation. Our questions form in the shape of the testings we experience: "Why me? Why us? Haven't I/we suffered enough?"

Several years ago my family and I were in Mexico for a vacation. We were visiting some of Lucy's family in Cabo San Lucas at the tip of Baja California. On a warm, sunny day we had gone to the beach to do some swimming and snorkeling. My two daughters and I were out in the water bobbing around, and we decided that we would swim around the promontory of rocks that formed one side of the cove we were in. Both of my daughters are excellent swimmers, and I'm a decent one. My eldest daughter swam on ahead and the youngest, ten years old at the time, stayed close by my side. About three-fourths of the way out to the tip of the point, the rocks that formed the one side of the cove divided, with a space of twenty or so feet in between. I was winded and beginning to tire, so I decided to cut through the gap between the rocks and save myself thirty or so extra yards of swimming.

As I started through the opening between the rocks, I looked beneath the surface only to see the boiling, swirling maelstrom of the sea caused by a large formation of rock jutting up from the bottom but not quite reaching the top. I stopped and began frantically stroking in the opposite direction.

My youngest daughter, who was swimming immediately behind me, bumped into me and looked beneath the surface as well. She, too, saw the danger and began swimming in the opposite direction; all the while the sea tried to suck us down into the turbulence.

We managed to swim ourselves out of danger and continued around the point and eventually made it to the shore on the other side. I crawled the last few steps through the surf on my hands and knees, collapsing on the sand from exhaustion.

Shannon, my daughter who had been a part of the near disaster, sat down at my side. She had trusted her father implicitly and was ready to follow him wherever he took her. She believed that her father would never lead her into temptation, that he would never put her in a position where she couldn't make it.

I sat there in the warmth of the sun and in the safety of the shore, absolutely exhausted, thinking to myself that I almost hadn't made it. In the process I had almost taken my daughter with me. As I gasped for breath, she looked me in the eye and said, "Daddy, you almost swam us into a hole, didn't you? But you didn't. I guess God was with us, wasn't he?" Though her father had led her into temptation, her heavenly Father had mercifully intervened.

For some reason unknown to us, we are to ask the Father not to place us in the same position I had placed my daughter, a place of testing that would be more than she could handle. I believe the petition is there not for his sake but for ours, to remind us of our need of his direction and our need of his support.

Let me make several suggestions as to why we are tested.

God tests us *to expose the dross.* Testing brings to the surface those facets of our character and coping mechanisms which are inconsistent with his will. The example of my swimming shortcut comes to mind. As I sat there in the wet sand, I couldn't help but think about my impulsiveness and lack of judgment. I also became aware of the serious implications of my actions. Fathers don't act alone; very special people are involved in and implicated by our decisions.

The second reason is related to the first. We are tested *so that we might learn a lesson.* I am a professor in a graduate institution. When I give an exam, several purposes coalesce at the time of the test. The test measures what the students have learned and thus forms the basis for their grades. At the same time, the test itself becomes a learning experience. So it is sometimes when we are tested. The testing itself becomes a learning experience, and we profit from it.

Testing is meant *to help us identify our strengths.* You never know how much you can handle until you have been asked to handle more than you thought you could. Our human tendency is to opt for the conservative side of our experience rather than to choose to be tested.

For instance, if your sports team consistently plays teams who are less skilled and/or less competent than yours, you'll never know how good or bad you really are. When you play a team that is better than you are, you find out your strengths. Often you're better than you think, but you just had never been tested.

A fourth reason has to do with our ability *to respond to others who are being tested.* The apostle Paul wrote to the Corinthians that God comforts us in all our affliction "so that we can comfort those in any trouble with the comfort we ourselves have received from God" (2 Cor 1:4). When you've been through it yourself, whatever the "it" may be, you can sympathize with the pain and struggle of the one who is being tested. Of course, to value this reason, you must have a servant's attitude.

The difficulty with the reasons I've given so far is that some testings, such as death and terrible disease, don't seem to accrue benefits equal to the expenses involved. The gain is not worth the loss. Only a fifth reason is worth the expense. It is the most compelling reason we are tested: *to glorify the Father.*

The life of Job handsomely illustrates this fifth purpose behind testing. For some reason, Job's attitude toward the Father became a point of dispute between God and his former archangel, Satan. The question "Have you considered my servant Job?" (Job 1:8) lingers hauntingly over the story of Job and the tragedies of his life. Somehow Job's tenacious belief in God and his declaration, "Though he slay me, yet will I hope in him" (Job 13:15), glorified the Father.

According to this line of reasoning, each human being is part of a compelling drama and conflict between God and Satan. If one believer who is being tested to the limit chooses not to curse God and die, then the Father has been glorified. We're here not only for ourselves, not only for our usefulness, but especially to glorify the Father.

This conflict between God and Satan brings us to the second part of our request: "deliver us from evil."

Grace and Our Fallen Nature

According to James 1:14, evil isn't always a black cloud that stalks us; evil comes from within ourselves: "each one is tempted when, by his own evil desire, he is dragged away and enticed" (1:14). It's a matter, again, of the locus of control. When we are tempted, we are tempted of our own accord.

Admittedly, this is not much comfort. I can hear most of you saying: "Great. That's just what I needed to hear. I'm responsible for everything that goes wrong in my life. Some comfort. No wonder we're all cynics."

I can understand such a response. My answer is to question our interpretation of the idea of evil and our response to our evil sides. For many of us, these issues strike at the heart of our struggle to love God. Because we cannot accept our own evil, we must place the responsibility for it somewhere. Logically, that "somewhere" would be to put it back on God's shoulders.

We are now in a double bind. We know God can't or isn't supposed to be responsible for evil. It must be us. If he's all good, we must be all bad, and who wants to be all bad? The choice, on the surface, is between hating him or hating ourselves.

God loves us knowing that as Christians we possess simultaneously within ourselves the capacity for both good and evil. The great reformer Martin Luther said it best. He said we are *"simul sanctus et pecatur."* We are "simultaneously saint and sinner."

Evil does exist, and it does exist within us. We've got a problem—especially if we think in "either/or" terms rather than "both/and" terms. Dualists tend to sort the world into only two categories: good or bad, right or wrong, up or down, east or west. Dualism, a cultural heritage from our Greek intellectual roots, works against us when we need to accept our ambivalence. Ambivalence is the presence of two apparently different feelings existing inside us at the same time. The solution is to change our dualistic thinking and to accept that we are "simultaneously saints and sinners," simultaneously both good *and* evil, rather than good *or* evil.

But what shall we do with our evil side?

I suggest an alternative way of thinking about the whole issue of our inner evil. It is to think of ourselves as having both a light side and a dark side to our personalities. The light side of our personalities is everything we like about ourselves. Whatever we can comfortably embrace. In contrast, the dark side of our personalities is everything we don't like about ourselves. From the perspective of Scripture, the dark side is the evil part of ourselves, the part of ourselves that is sinful.

It's not hard to decide what to do with the light side of ourselves. We can embrace it and encourage it. Our problem is what to do with the dark side.

The most common human strategy is to split the good off from the bad and project it on someone else. In the same way a projector projects an image onto a screen, we can project our own evil onto others. We can't accept the dark side of ourselves, so we try to throw it away.

Projection is one explanation for our blaming and defensive tendencies. We blame others for the dark side of ourselves rather than take responsibility for it. The struggle with our dark side makes us defensive and sensitive.

We're not alone. I believe the apostle Paul's struggle with his dark side provoked him to cry out, "What a wretched man I am! Who will rescue me from this body of death?" (Rom 7:24). Throughout his writings, Paul spoke of the tension between his two natures constantly at war with one another. We can sympathize with Paul because we can feel the struggle he felt.

According to this way of looking at ourselves, we cannot become comfortable with ourselves as mature people until we find some way to accept our "dark sides." Yet, how can we become comfortable with our "dark sides" without compromising our standards as Christians? If we are to be delivered from evil, and the evil is within us, what shall we do?

Remember that Jesus came and gave his life for us on the cross because of the evil side of our characters and personalities. He died for our dark sides. Therefore, we can accept the dark side of ourselves because of the righteousness of Christ.

He doesn't make the evil into good; it's still within us. He doesn't change the dark into light. That's perfectionism. He does make us acceptable to God. Because we're acceptable to God, we can accept ourselves.

This acceptance of ourselves because of our relationship with Christ is what mercy and grace are all about. We can take responsibility for ourselves and for our dark sides because we have confidence that the Father has embraced us in Christ. We can confidently say with the apostle Paul, "Therefore, there is now no condemnation for those who are in Christ Jesus" (Rom 8:1). We are free of all condemnation—from God, from others and from ourselves. It's much easier to love God when we are "free indeed."

Resisting the Evil One

Many New Testament translators believe the phrase *deliver us from evil* would be better translated as *deliver us from the evil one*. In one sense the issue is merely academic because to be delivered from evil would include deliverance from the power of Satan. Either way we still need to know how to deal with our own evil as well as deal with "the evil one."

The Lord's Prayer assumes that Satan exists as a real being. He is the prince of the power of the air. He is the god of this world. Because he exists we must take his presence into account. He has influence but he isn't omnipresent. He isn't God. The tendency in today's world is either to give Satan greater credit than is due him or to ignore him completely.

Whatever his status, Jesus was particularly aware of Satan's ability both to tempt and to test. Jesus' experience in the wilderness was fresh in his mind as he taught his disciples to pray. I'm sure his experience with the presence of Satan prompted him to encourage his disciples to pray, "But deliver us from the evil one."

Whatever we choose to think about Satan, we shouldn't discount his power. For those who give him opportunity, he can control and dominate. For those who ignore him, he can seduce and influence. For those who fear him, he can control them through their fear.

The believer must resist Satan, whose power is only as great as we allow it to be. His greatest power comes in his ability to discourage us.

Scripture, especially Job, teaches us that Satan's discouragement comes from several sources: circumstances, as well as misguided information, advice and criticism.

The circumstances in Job's life were shattering. He had lost his children, possessions and health. He was destitute and vulnerable. Into the vacuum created by his experience, Satan influenced Job's friends in the advice and criticism they heaped on him.

Far from comforting him, his friends told Job there was sin in his life, that he was a misguided fool. They were the final straw designed to break him. Those who knew him best could hurt him the worst.

In terms of Satan's power to hinder us from loving God, the failure of those closest to us to be loving and supportive is Satan's greatest tool. We can stand almost anything except being alone.

The final blow to Job's defenses was the desertion of his friends when he really needed them. Satan's ultimate manipulation was the backbiting, criticism and gossiping of those who knew Job best. The presence and absence of supportive friends can be the critical issue tipping the scales of our trust in God one way or another.

In spite of the ultimate loss of those who were supposed to

love him, Job still remained faithful to God. In his commitment, God was glorified. God promises to stand with us against Satan in the same way he comforted Job.

We tend to romanticize testing, whether testing by circumstances or Satanic attack. Novels and sermon illustrations gloss over the very real pain experienced by those who are being tested. The Hollywood scenario of violence without pain is repeated all in the name of God.

According to my experience and observation, our faith in God in no way exempts us from the pain, struggle, loss and grief endemic to all human persons. The promise of God is that whatever our circumstance, whatever our testing, and however we are attacked, we can know the love of Christ in the worst of times. We will never be alone. He will be our Shepherd and our Staff, our shelter and our support.

He will not be a narcotic to shield us from the pain. Because we are human we are vulnerable to all that is common to our humanity—including testing. Because we are human we will be attacked.

The Father's love will sustain us whatever the circumstances and whatever the cost. The Son will put his enemies under his feet in the here and now, as he will put them under his feet in eternity. Thus, will the Son be vindicated and the Father glorified.

Our Trust and a Loving God

It's tough to love God when you're being tested. It's even harder to love God when that testing takes the form of Satanic attack. All the while we can know God's love for us, even if at the moment we don't love him. His love is not predicated upon our performance nor upon our perseverance. His faithfulness will outlast ours. In the midst of testing several simple declarative statements hold true:

☐ *We can trust the Father to know and understand us.* In high school I had a football coach who pushed us at times beyond what seemed to be our breaking point. I can remember being totally exhausted and the coach yelling at us to "suck it up and dig a little harder." He always wanted more.

Then, on one very hot, smoggy September afternoon, we walked onto the field dreading what lay ahead. We were geared up for the torture of an afternoon practice made worse by heat and smog. Much to our surprise, the coach ran us through a light workout and then turned us loose to go home early.

On the way back to the gym, several of the seniors were walking with him. Someone asked him why he was letting us off so easy. He replied that we wouldn't last fifteen minutes in the heat, and the smog just made it worse. He knew our limits and wasn't going to push us just for the sake of breaking us. He seemed to know what we could handle and what we couldn't. He understood us.

If a coach can know that about his players, how much more does the Father who is in heaven know about his children? He will neither push us less than we should be pushed nor more than we can handle.

☐ *We can trust the Father to want the best for us.* The Father's love has integrity. God is not capricious. He's not out to "get" us. His love doesn't exempt us from the down side of our humanity, but it does support us when we need it the most.

Because of our past experience with the people in our lives, trusting God to want the best for us is one of the harder tasks we face. It is important to remember that his love for us is not contingent upon our response to him. We didn't earn his love. It has been given freely but not cheaply. Neither can we keep his love. It is maintained freely but not cheaply. The death of the Son on the cross was the full price to be paid to earn the Father's love.

The faithful intercession of the Son in heaven on our behalf is the full reason we persevere. Wanting the best for us involved saving us and it involves keeping us. We are the valued-though-unworthy recipients of his grace and his mercy. Because of Christ we can know the Father, and because of Christ we can love him.

☐ *We can trust the Father to accept us in spite of our dark side.* The poet Robert Frost once wrote:

Home is the place where, when you have to go there,

They have to take you in.

Home involves an unconditional acceptance based on relationship and not on performance. Your family are the ones who know the worst about you. Yet, in the best sense of the word, they are the ones who welcome you back in spite of your failures and with full knowledge of your shortcomings.

So it is with the Father. Nothing about our dark side surprises him. He knows the secret places of our hearts. He knows the images of lust, the fantasies of grandeur, the small snippets of hate and bitterness known only to us and unknown to all else. Like the seeming omniscient parent, he knows what's going on inside the door of our bedroom before he knocks and the door is opened.

Still, because of our relationship with his Son, he loves and accepts us. The Son has made the way to the Father open, and he keeps the way to the Father straight. There is no confusion. We have all gone astray. It is only because of the Father's love for us in Christ that we can call him Father. It is only because of his grace and mercy that we persist. He died for us knowing the worst about us, and he intercedes in heaven for us knowing our weaknesses and our sin. For God there are no surprises nor secrets.

☐ *We can trust the Father to triumph over Satan.* If anything, Satan is a bully. As is the case of any bully, when stood up to he will run and hide. As we pray the Lord's Prayer we can be certain that the God of heaven will triumph over the god of the earth. According to Scripture, the battle has been fought and the outcome determined by the obedience of the Son. Like us, Christ's obedience became a "cause celebre" to glorify his Father. Because of his obedience we too will triumph.

We have many reasons to trust the Father to whom we pray. Granted, the reasons are not always tangible nor are they concrete. However, they have been tested in the laboratory of human experience by those who have been tested before us. For those who trust in God, the pain may be the same as the pain is for those who don't trust, but the meaning beneath the pain will be different because trusting brings glory to the Father. The Father will give "the crown of life that God has promised to those who love him" (Jas 1:12).

In plain and simple words, we love God for his sake and not for ours. In this way the Father is glorified, and we, as his children, are fulfilled.

CHAPTER THIRTEEN

A CLOSING HYMN

*F*or thine is the kingdom, and the power, and the glory, for ever. Amen."

The closing stanzas of the great hymns of the faith are usually as compelling as are the first. Whether it's "O for a Thousand Tongues" or "Fairest Lord Jesus," the magnificence of the last verse usually matches the grandeur of the first. The case of the Lord's Prayer should be no exception.

Perhaps that's why the phrase *For thine is the kingdom, and the power, and the glory, for ever. Amen.* found its way into the text. According to the earliest copies of the Greek New Testament, this phrase was not in the original text or part of Jesus' instruction to his disciples. Most responsible scholars of the New Testament agree the phrase was added later.

If this is so, why was it included?

The Lord's Prayer became central to the worship of the early church and probably became the text of a hymn sung by small groups of gathered believers. When they came together, they likely celebrated the Lord's Supper as Jesus had instructed them, and they sang or chanted the Lord's words as they remembered them. The Lord's Prayer from Matthew's Gospel had become a central part of their worship experience.

While transcribing Matthew's Gospel carefully by hand, one of the early copyists probably decided that the words in the text he was copying from had something missing. He had sung the prayer before in worship, and the text before him omitted a phrase that was in the hymn, so he included it as a part of his text. For whatever reason, the phrase *for thine is the kingdom, and the power, and the glory, for ever. Amen.* found its way into the text at a later date. It became a part of the worship of the church from that point on.

Irrespective of the textual controversies, in a way I agree with the copyist who included it, because it finishes off the prayer with the spirit of worship the prayer deserves. It is the last verse of a magnificent hymn. Because the phrase has become such a part of our worship experience, and the worship experiences of generations of gathered believers, it's fitting to finish our discussion with these words in mind.

The Kingdom

The concept of the kingdom of God is at the center of the prayer, as it is at the center of the purpose underlying the prayer. Understanding that purpose is the beginning of what it means to love God. Embracing that purpose is what it means to mature in one's love.

The kingdom of God in its here-and-now and its yet-to-come

dimensions places demands on us concerning who and what we are now and who and what we are becoming.

If we embrace the concept of the kingdom of God, it reminds us of *the Father's right to rule*. We are his people, and he is our God. We are to have no other gods before him. His commandments are clear. The Father is to be worshiped as the ultimate claimant on our lives.

It's possible to worship a god because you fear him and not because you love him. The compelling message of the Lord's Prayer is that the God of the kingdom is worthy to be loved because he loves us. He can be trusted because he has created a time and a place for us. He is neither detached from us nor is he our adversary. He is "for us" rather than against us. We are encouraged, rather than commanded, to come into his presence. He preserves our dignity as his created beings as he listens to our petitions. The God of the kingdom is our Father.

The concept of the kingdom of God focuses not only on the Father's rule, it focuses as well on *the Father's kingdom*. The ideal of "realm" has to do with the sphere of the ruler's dominion.

This is "our Father's world." It is not ours. It is not ours to use irresponsibly nor is it ours to despoil. The majesty and the beauty of his creation are linked together in the symmetry of the eco-system. Like a Calder mobile, the pieces of our environment hang precariously balanced in time and space.

We are his viceregents given dominion over his world, yet we strip-mine his hillsides, we ravage his rain forests, and we poke holes in the ozone layers of his atmosphere—all in the name of progress. The animals we were to name are slaughtered for fur coats. The fields we were to till are poisoned with chemicals. The rivers and seas created on the second day are polluted with toxic waste. We mask with "technological advances" our greed and our insatiable appetites for luxury. We live out our lives as if the world were ours and not his.

The manner in which we treat our environment has become a metaphor of our relationship to the kingdom of God. We treat it as if it's an issue to be debated and not a stewardship to be preserved. What's amazing to me are the theological debates and the well-crafted sermons dedicated to the *idea* of the kingdom of God, while the *reality* of God's kingdom—the planet on which we live and expect Jesus' return—is neglected as if it doesn't exist. How is it that we can believe in the reality of his kingdom and neglect the realm of his kingdom?

I don't intend this to be a lecture on environmental issues, though I do believe that when we speak of his kingdom we must take responsibility for what we can control. The realm of his kingdom does include the people who live here and the planet on which we live. God loves the people who populate his kingdom and for some inscrutable reason he loves the place they live. Loving God involves loving those he loves and the places they live.

The Power

When we think of power we usually think of it in the same way we think of strength. If people are powerful they are strong. They may be physically powerful or they may be powerful in the sense that they can control what happens. This has to do with *power* in the coercive sense of the word. In this sense, when we think of God as being powerful, it is his bigness and his might we are referring to.

Power has other connotations as well. *Power* can refer to the ability to influence others. The one who is being influenced can choose to be influenced or not. God's power in the present is limited by his choice to give us choices. Because we are created in his image, we have been given the freedom to choose, the power to be powerful. When we pray "for thine is the power," though that power will be absolute in the future, we are recognizing the contingent nature of God's power in the present.

Power can also refer to the ability to control the resources we have. Thus, a wife and mother may be submissive to her husband, but if she controls the resources available to the family she has power.

God's power, as delineated in the Lord's Prayer, has reference to his control of the resources available to us. He is the one who metes out "our daily bread." Our recognition of his control of our resources reminds us of our stewardship of his resources. He gives to us what he wants us to take care of for him: ourselves, our children, our possessions, our environment. Loving God in this sense of the word is tangible and concrete. It's something we *do* rather than something we *feel*. Loving God involves taking care of all that he has left in our care.

The Glory

On the night the Savior was born, the shepherds heard a heavenly chorus of angels singing "glory to God in the highest." They returned to their fields "glorifying and praising God for all the things they had heard and seen" (Lk 2:20).

The glory of God is at the heart of our worship. It is what we have fallen short of because we are sinners. God's glory is the worship due him because of who he is and because of what he has done.

The glory of God is what provokes awe in us when we contemplate his greatness. It is the chill that runs up our backs when we hear Handel's "Hallelujah Chorus." It is the wonder we feel when we ponder the tiny and fully formed fingers of an infant asleep in our arms. It is the insignificance we experience when we stand in the spray of Niagara Falls, hearing the roar of the cascading water and seeing the boiling foam of the falling river.

The glory of God is the respect that is due him because he sent his Son to become a human being. It is the paradox of the Incarnation: What shouldn't have happened, did. God became a man. It is the response we feel when we discover his love and justice satisfied by the Son's death on the cross. It's the swelling we experience within our chests when we sing of Christ's resurrection on an Easter morn.

Sometimes it's hard to love God because the lens of our experience focuses our attention on ourselves and not on him. Attractive and seductive gods compete for our worship. The natural narcissism of our age legitimatizes our self-centeredness. The arrogance of our culture teaches us to place ourselves at the center of the universe.

The glory of God is the antidote to the poison of our self-aggrandisement. It is our response to his countenance. The glory of God is what ultimately provokes us to love him.

For Ever

Forever is, as the King James Version states it, *for ever.* That's a long time. In fact, it's further than tomorrow, because you can't see beyond it. It never quits. Only God, himself, can understand its meaning. We can speak the word and describe its qualities, but we only experience it as a shadow. Its reality and intent are beyond us.

When we sing the hymn, the word *forever* is the intent of our heart that our worship should never end. *Forever* is the line that extends as far into the future as we can imagine, only to surface again behind us when we contemplate the mighty works of God in the past. *Forever* is the gift of eternal life we receive in Christ and the mystery of eternity itself. *Forever* is the length, the width, the breadth and the depth of the Father's love for us, whether or not we are able to love him back. *Forever* never ends.

Amen

The word *amen* is the Hebrew word for "so be it." It's like an exclamation point at the end of a spirited conversation. In terms of loving God, whether it is hard or confusing or simple, the *amen* is our agreement that we are willing to "let it begin and let it begin with me." When we speak the *amen* at the end of the prayer it marks both the end of the prayer and the beginning of our commitment.

As we end our discussion together, I simply invite you as an act of worship to join me in the saying of the prayer. Know that when you pray, the Father who hears, accepts your prayer in whatever state you are in and for whatever reason you pray. Let's end this book as he taught us to pray . . .

Our Father which art in heaven,
Hallowed be thy name.
Thy kingdom come.
Thy will be done in earth, as it is in heaven.
Give us this day our daily bread.
And forgive us our debts,
as we forgive our debtors.
And lead us not into temptation,
but deliver us from evil:
For thine is the kingdom,
and the power, and the glory,
for ever. Amen (Mt 6:9-13 KJV)